The First 100 Years of Scouting
in the Narragansett Council

The First 100 Years of Scouting in the Narragansett Council

(A collection of accounts from many different sources.)

authorHOUSE®

AuthorHouse™ LLC
1663 Liberty Drive
Bloomington, IN 47403
www.authorhouse.com
Phone: 1-800-839-8640

Published by AuthorHouse   07/10/2013

ISBN: 978-1-4817-7520-5 (sc)
ISBN: 978-1-4817-7516-8 (e)

Library of Congress Control Number: 2013912522

INTRODUCTION
to
"The First One Hundred Years of Scouting in the Narragansett Council"

While this book certainly does not cover all events, name all volunteers or staff members or represent all units, it does represent a general history of the Narragansett Council.

The material provided herein is a combination of information from several history books, minutes of Executive Board meetings and the memories of staff and volunteers. Some of the material included in this history book may be repetitive as each source may have touched on the same material. Listed below are the sources of this information.

"Scout Trail 1910-1962", by J. Harold Williams

"High Tides in Rhode Island Scouting", by J. Harold Williams

"25 Years of Scouting in Rhode Island" by G. Edward Buxton and J. Harold Williams

"Yawgoog's History Milestones", Internet

Many thanks to everyone who contributed to the compilation, writing and editing of this history.

*David S. Anderson, former Scout Executive from 2000 to 2011

Vincent N. Borrelli, former Scout Executive from 1973 to 1990

Jules A. Cohen, Past President Narragansett Council and current Board Member

Andrew M. Erickson, Past President Narragansett Council and current Board Member

Judy A. Ferrante, Administrative Assistant from 1983 to Present

Eric Creamer, Service Area Director from 2007 to Present

Diane J. Cloutier, Service Area Staff Member, 2000 to Present

Jonathan P. Widmark, Development Director, 2006 to Present

Over the Hill Gang Members for their proofreading skills.

Scoutmasters and Leaders who provided information on Unit Histories

*This book is dedicated in Memory of David S. Anderson.

A BRIEF HISTORY OF THE NARRAGANSETT COUNCIL AND THE RHODE ISLAND BOY SCOUTS (RIBS)

Narragansett Council, Boy Scouts of America is part of a worldwide Scouting movement with over 15 million members in one hundred countries. Boy Scouting began in England in 1907 when the British military hero, Lord Robert Baden-Powell, organized the first Boy Scout camp. In 1908, he published Scouting for Boys and formed what would become the British Boy Scout Association.

The Scouting Program, in the territory served by Narragansett Council, is administered by two corporations, Narragansett Council, BSA and Rhode Island Boy Scouts. The dual corporation is rare in the Boy Scouts of America and can be confusing to new members to the organization. The simple explanation is that Narragansett Council is the Operating organization holding a Charter from the Boy Scouts of America and RIBS receives, holds and administers the physical assets of the Council in cooperation with the Executive Board of the Council. To understand how it works, it is necessary to understand the history of both organizations.

Scouting in Rhode Island was formalized as the Rhode Island Boy Scouts when, responding to the significant interest in the greater Providence area, Charles E. Mulhearn and Colonel G. Edward Buxton, Jr. formed a State Scout Committee on September 6, 1910 at the Rhode Island State House. The State Committee, under the leadership of Col. Mulhearn as Chief Scout (President) of the Rhode Island Boy Scouts, appointed Col. Buxton to be Scout Commissioner, Rowland G. Hazard, Commissioner from Washington County, and Adjutant General Charles W; Abbot, Jr., Commissioner for Bristol County. By October 24th the first five Boy Scout Troops were organized and a Scout Headquarters was opened in the *Journal* Building. On April 13, 1911, RIBS was chartered under state laws for the purpose of giving boys of Rhode Island an organization in which they could be formed into groups that mirrored the newly formed national Boy Scout Program. The Incorporators included Judge Patrick P. Curran, George W. Gardiner, George Leland Miner, Judge Howard B. Gorham, State Treasurer Walter A. Read, Col. Harry Cutler, Frank W. Matteson, Walter Callender, James H. Higghins, Edgar R. Barker, E. Merle Bixby, Harris H. Bucklin, Stuart Campbell, T. F. I. McDonnell, Edward A. Stockwell, Harold L. Madison and John R. Rathom. John R. Rathom, editor of the Providence Journal, became Scout Commissioner in 1911 and was instrumental in giving Scouting its driving force and character during its early years.

In the very beginning (1910) Scout units were organized by individuals who had read or heard of Baden Powell's "Scouting for Boys" program. One of the original handbooks is on display at the Alumni Museum at Yawgoog Scout Reservation in Rockville, Rhode Island. Soon, other men and boys became interested and here and across the nation, Boy Scout Troops began to form. It soon became clear that there was a need for leader training, camp assistance and other administrative help to keep the program attractive to boys. In the Greater Providence area, there was great interest in the program and on April 13th 1910, the Rhode Island Boy Scouts was incorporated under the laws of the State of Rhode Island led by Charles E. Mulhern and G. Edward Buxton, Jr.

From 1910 to 1917, Rhode Island Boy Scouts established groups (Troops) throughout Rhode Island, except in Newport, the Blackstone Valley and Woonsocket. In these locations, Troops were organized and affiliated with the National Council, Boy Scouts of America. While the Rhode Island Boy Scouts were getting underway, Scouting was taking root in Newport and Pawtucket under the auspices of the Boy Scouts of America, which had been incorporated on February 8, 1910. Ernest Thompson Seton, Chief Scout of the Boy Scouts of America, had lectured in Newport in the summer of 1910. This resulted in a meeting in 1911 at the home of Mrs. John Nicholas Brown leading to the formation of a Boy Scouts of America Council in Newport by Major Lorillard Spencer, Superintendent of Schools Lull, Austin L. Sands, A. R. C. Gatzenmeier and others. Soon after, in Pawtucket, Andrew Meiklejohn, Robert Johnston, Albert L. Copeland, and Thomas A. Holt started the first Scout Troops. A Boy Scouts of America Council was chartered in Pawtucket in 1916. Woonsocket also went its own way and formed a separate Council in 1924.

While the Boy Scouts of America was in the process of organizing nationally, the Rhode Island Boy Scouts was not a council of the BSA. The movement was bringing together at least two organizations that were using Baden Powell's program and at the same time, it was organizing into ten regions or territories to administer the program of the Boy Scouts of America. On February 8th, 1910, the BSA received its charter from Congress and began to move forward with its organization. In the meantime things were moving along in the Greater Providence area. New troops were formed, an executive was hired and the first purchases were made at Yawgoog. Scouting was flourishing. RIBS was officially organized on September 6th, 1910, and from 1910 to 1917 troops were established throughout Rhode Island except in Newport, the Black-tone Valley and Woonsocket. Troops in these areas were organized and affiliated with the National Council.

In 1916, RIBS acquired a permanent camp site of 130 acres on Yawgoog Pond in the Town of Hopkinton. The land was part of the Palmer Farm and the purchase price was $1,500. Additional property acquisitions were made in 1932, 1935 and 1951, which brought the Yawgoog holdings to 800 acres. Today Yawgoog acreage encompasses over 1,800 acres.

Early days at Yawgoog—winter hiking and camping

The Boy Scout wave, swelling out from Lord Robert Baden-Powell's first Scout camp on Brownsea Island in 1907 swept into Rhode Island in 1910. It brought together early in the year four Newport boys at the home of Harold C. Warden, one of the number to form a patrol. It caused square-jawed 17 year old Milton R. MacIntosh to "organize a troop" in the spring among the Eddy Street gangs of South Providence. It started with a dozen or more boys meeting a little later in Washington Park under the leadership of Deputy Superintendent of Police John A. Murray.

In September, 1910, the first sponsoring organization was formed and the Washington Park unit was recognized as the First Providence Troop with a membership of 64 Scouts and with Herbert R. Dean, a young cavalryman, as the first Scoutmaster in the State. Milton MacKintosh's group in South Providence was recognized as the Second Providence Troop. The Third Providence Troop on the East Side was led by Prescott Lovell. Charles R. Stark, Jr., was Scoutmaster of the Fourth Providence Troop in the Dexter Parade Ground area and the Fifth Providence Troop was at the Boys' Club under Scoutmaster John Kelly, who later became Superintendent of Police. Dr. Max B. Gomberg formed a Troop on Benefit Street, of which Veteran Scouter Walter Adler was a charter member. Dr. Raymond F. Hacking was referred to as 'the first Boy Scout' because he was the "First Sergeant" (Senior Patrol Leader) of the First Providence Troop, which has continued with unbroken service ever since 1910, the only one of the original troops to do so. Troops were also being organized in Cranston, East Providence, North Providence, Warwick, Bristol and Washington County. Some Scoutmasters from those early years were Grafton I. Kenyon at Wakefield, Edward L. Waterman at Conimicut, Arthur L. Lake at Allendale, George R. Fish at Bristol, Dr. Patrick J. Manning at Wickford, George B. Utter, Robert C. Thackery, Silas T. Nye at Westerly and T. Dawson Brown at Six Corners.

As a result of a "good turn" performed by an English Scout in London for Chicago publisher William D. Boyce, Scouting gained greater publicity in America. The Boy Scouts of America was incorporated in 1910 and chartered by Congress on June 15, 1916.

During its first three years, the movement attained a membership of approximately 2,000, but hard times set in. The organization began to lose ground in 1914 and 1915, as the first wave of enthusiasm was wearing off. Leadership training methods were inadequate, the lack of a printed Manual was felt and funds were scarce. The volunteers directing the State and county organizations found it hard to give the time needed to keep troops going; to replace leaders; to form new troops. By the beginning of 1916, the membership had fallen to approximately 500. There was bickering among Scoutmasters, few activities, and affairs reached a crisis. Mr. Rathom and the State group decided that a full-time paid executive was needed and Col. Buxton was chairman of the committee which brought to Rhode Island from Springfield, Massachusetts, Donald North, a graduate of Springfield College, to be the executive. Mr. North who had been in Boys' Club and probation work, took up his duties early in 1916 and he soon won the affection and allegiance of the leaders. Things began to boom again as Don North was a promoter. The organization raised money, two little Manuals were printed, Scoutmasters' lectures were arranged and Mr. North made speeches all over the state. Donald North was a 'three-year-on-a-job" man and resigned in 1918. He went on to become Superintendent of the Rhode Island Training School for Boys at Sockanosset. Later he left to become the Scout Executive of Boston and then returned to Rhode Island to be Chief Probation Officer. He died in that office in 1937. Donald North Court at Yawgoog is named in his memory.

Scouts helping during the Flu Pandemic

Another significant event of 1911 was the development in Rhode Island of a new magazine, "Boys' Life," labeled by 18-year old Joseph Lane, its founder, as "the official Boy Scout magazine". On July 19, 1912, the Boy Scouts of America purchased it and really made it the official publication of the Boy Scouts of America. The first distributor of Scouting uniforms and equipment was The Outlet Company. The uniform consisted of a little 'campaign' hat with a big tin Eagle and R.I.B.S. on the front, a little high-necked khaki jacket, khaki breeches and leggings attached, and a tiny haversack about big enough for a sandwich and a pickle.

The first long-term camping took place in the summer of 1911 on Prudence Island in June and early July. In August, the Rhode Island Boy Scouts conducted a big camp in Greystone, directed by Scoutmaster Stark. In 1912 and 1913, the Scouts camped on Col. Rodman's Kettle Hole Pond property in Allenton and in 1914 and 1915 on Mount Hope through the generosity of the late R. F. Haffenreffer, Jr. The Greystone camp was followed by Camp Rodman in 1912 and 1913 at Kettle Hole Pond, Allenton. Williams never forgot "the long hike from the cars at Wickford; the tents on the hill top; the evening parade and the dish washing in the cold water of the brook." The next organization camp was on Mount Hope during 1914 and 1915, through the courtesy of R. F. Haffenreffer, Jr. The camping technique was improving some. They had warm water to wash dishes in. Mount Hope was a very charming camp and among his papers was a faded newspaper page of the *Sunday Journal* feature section in which Williams contributed an article on "A Rhode Island Boy Scout's Experiences on Mount Hope."

At the waterfront, Camp Yawgoog

On May 22nd, 1917, Rhode Island Boy Scouts and the Boy Scouts of America reached an agreement under which the Greater Providence Council Boy Scouts of America was formed to take over the operation of the Scouting program and supervision of Troops. The National Council of the Boy Scouts of America recognized the date of the Council's organization as September 6th, 1910 and granted all members back service to that date. The National Council also agreed that the Rhode Island Boy Scouts could maintain its corporate identity so that it could continue to receive bequests, hold funds and properties and acquire other assets for Scouting's benefit in the future. Thus, today there are two separate Scouting organizations in our area. Narragansett Council is an operating entity (which leases its camps from the Rhode Island Boy Scouts) and the Rhode Island Boy Scouts which acts as a corporate trustee.

In 1918, Captain George Bucklin, a war veteran who had lived in Texas for several years and was formerly from East Providence, Rhode Island, died. Upon his death, Captain Bucklin made the Rhode Island Boy Scouts the chief beneficiary under his will, which was to be administered by the Rhode Island Hospital Trust Company. The estate was worth $750,000 at that time. The will provided that a building for the Rhode Island Boy Scouts use was to be erected and that any income over that necessary for insurance, repairs, taxes and expenses of maintenance, should be paid to the Rhode Island Boy Scouts for its general use. To that end, in 1931, the trust constructed the Bucklin Memorial on property given to it by the Rhode Island Boy Scouts at Camp Yawgoog.

On December 15th, 1918, 21-year old J. Harold Williams became the Scout Executive and Camp Chief of Yawgoog. He gave up his job as a *Providence Journal* reporter and Scoutmaster of the Third Providence Troop. The National Council would only accept him as 'Acting Executive', membership was down to 1,000 and payrolls were hard to meet. Young Williams flourished under great leadership: Council President T. F I. McDonnell, George L. Gross, chairman of the Executive Committee, Richard S. Aldrich as Treasurer and Col Buxton. In the 1920's the Providence Journal needed the space in their building so the Rhode Island Boy Scouts moved to the Strand Building. Then in the early thirties, the office was moved to 100 North Main Street and in the late thirties moved again to 26 Custom House Street. In 1957 the building was sold to be torn down and Headquarters again moved, this time to the Caesar Misch Building at 51 Empire Street. It wasn't until September 20, 1964, that the new Council Service Center on 175 Broad Street in Providence was dedicated. After 40 years and many internal refurbishments, Scout Headquarters on Broad Street was sold in 2004 and Narragansett Council moved to improved quarters at 10 Risho Avenue in East Providence, where it is currently located.

1927 to 1933 has been referred to as 'The Brown Era', the era when T. Dawson Brown was President and the leader of Scouting. His biggest achievement was the purchase of the 800 acres of land surrounding Yawgoog Pond, and, in later years, the full and complete water rights to Yawgoog Pond and adjoining Wincheck Pond. In 1928 the enlarged Yawgoog property was dedicated and in his address Col. Buxton referred to Yawgoog as a *Scout Adventureland forever,* which is maintained still to this day. The Gateway to Yawgoog was originally named the Thunderbird Gate but was later named the T. Dawson Brown Gateway in memory of Brown. The gate was designed by F. Ellis Jackson and it features six totems, originally carved by sculptor Aristide Cianfarani. At the top are two Thunderbirds, which some Native Americans believed to be the messengers to the Great Spirit and protectors of campers. The remaining totems symbolize gifts that Scouts may receive when they enter: the Bear (Strength), the Fox (Woodcraft), the Beaver (Industry), and the Owl (Knowledge). The totems have been replaced over the years, but the originals can be found in the Bucklin Memorial Building.

1931 Slumgullion at Yawgoog

Early years—Slumgullion at Yawgoog

In 1929 and 1930, the Greater Providence Council merged with the Newport County Council, the Pawtucket-Central Falls Council and the Woonsocket Council and changed its name to the Narragansett Council. In 1931, the Bucklin Memorial Building was erected on land at Yawgoog. The entire memorial, however, consists of a group of buildings around a quadrangle rather than a single building.

The Rhode Island Boy Scouts and the Narragansett Council separated that year and the operations of Scouting activities was turned over to the Narragansett Council. The Rhode Island Boy Scouts continued to own and hold Scouting properties, administer the Bucklin Trust income and all other bequests and gifts received. The relationship established in 1931 continues to exist today—all Scout properties are held by the RIBS and bequests and memorials created by donors are administered by RIBS. Donations are made to both the Narragansett Council and the Rhode Island Boy Scouts and the funds are invested as directed by the Investment Committee.

Also during the Brown era, in 1929 and 1930, the Greater Providence Council Boy Scouts of America merged with the Newport County Council, the Pawtucket-Central Falls Council and the Woonsocket Council to form the Narragansett Council. In May of 1930, a great forest fire started across the line in Connecticut, swept into Rhode Island and for three days devastated Yawgoog forest. Once the fire was out, Scouts cleared the affected areas and planted thousands of pine and spruce seedlings in the blackened acres soon after the conflagration and in years following and nature and time repaired the rest. The 1930's was the start of the Cub Scout Movement by the National Council for boys 9, 10 and 11. (Later when the minimum Boy Scout age was dropped to 11, the Cub Scout beginning age was lowered to 8). Leadership Training also took off in the 1930's beginning with the "University of Scouting", offering training for all ranks of leaders and for committeemen. It offered elementary training and advanced training, with a variety of courses in skills and in theory. The "University of Scouting" to this day, is still offered each year. Another good training tool which was first published on November 14, 1919, was "The Stalker", with the slogan "On the Trail of Ideas". It started as a single mimeographed sheet but grew to sometimes include 14 or 15 pages. In the nineties the name was changed to "Trail Signs" and as time went on and the new electronic age of computers came about, Scouting news, training and events are now transmitted via computer to our Scouting volunteers and families.

Sea Scouting was started in the early twenties in Rhode Island, following a visit from James A. Wilder, Chief Sea Scout, an Hawaiian-born Scouting enthusiast. For about 20 years this movement prospered and just prior to World War II, there were 25 ships and three hundred and fifty members registered, with cruises totaling 2417 miles, annual regattas and ceremonial Bridges of Honor. From 1930 to 1935, the Narragansett Council owned and operated the "Dolphin", a 43-foot Alden-built schooner but the limited number of boys who could be served each season and the high cost of operation forced the Council to sell her. Professor Edson I. Schock of the University of Rhode Island, a noted Naval Architect, created "The Narragansett Sea Scout", a 13-foot sailing dinghy, which would be built by the Sea Scout units themselves and which were sturdy and suitable for cruising on Narragansett Bay. The new boat caught on and 20 "Sea Scouts" were built locally but growth of Sea Scouting came to a halt with World War II. At this writing Narragansett Council has five active Sea Scouting units.

Here are several photos from the early 30's of the Dolphin
owned and operated by the Narragansett Council.

H. Cushman Anthony became a member of the Narragansett Council professional staff in 1927. "Gus", as he was affectionately known to everyone in Scouting, had many talents and was an organizer, administrator, camping director and Scoutcrafter who brought about increased membership and development of camping in Narragansett Council. He started work in Providence; went to Blackstone Valley to become executive of that district after its merger with Narragansett Council and returned to the Capital City and then became Assistant Scout Executive. He was J. Harold Williams' right-hand man and served the Narragansett Council from 1921 to 1969, when he retired from Professional Scouting. Staying close and involved with Scouting even in retirement, Gus established the Yawgoog Alumni Association in 1981 which includes members all throughout the United States and other countries such as Italy, Africa, Brazil, Switzerland, etc. In 1933, Gus married Jane Kiser and together they had one daughter, Gwen Anthony Mazanetz. Gus passed away on August 2nd, 2000, at the age of 96.

There was tremendous membership growth from 1935 to 1939 reaching a peak of 10,022 men and boys. This was due in large part to the endorsement of Scouting in 1935 as a program of the Roman Catholic Church by Most Rev. Francis P. Keough, Bishop of Providence. The growth ended with the beginning of World War II. Sixty per cent of Narragansett Council units lost their leaders and some of the units had as many as five and six different Scoutmasters during the war period. Transportation restrictions prevented any Council-wide meetings. There were no Jamborees, Pow-Wows, no mobilizations or council dinners. Membership picked up in 1944 and by the end of the year membership climbed to 12,535. Under the guidance of Rev. Earl Hollier Tomlin a Protestant Committee on Scouting, composed of clergymen and laymen, was formed. A Jewish Committee on Scouting was formed under the leadership of Jacob S. Temkin and Joseph Jacobson. The growing interest of the religious faiths in Scouting resulted in the dedication in 1948 of tracts of land at Yawgoog for religious use. On three different sites, Catholic, Protestants and Jews erected centers for worship.

LOCAL BOY SCOUTS — These young scouts were all prepared to journey to Camp Yawgoog in Rockville in 1936 when this photograph was taken. Left to right, were Charles Barker, George H. Utter, Charles Ferguson, Alex Ferguson, Donald Payne, John Walker, Bud Clarke and Phillip Greene. They were in Troop Three Westerly.

In honor of the many Scouts who entered active military service during World War II and for the 391 active and former Scouts who died "For God and Country", the bell in the memorial tower at Yawgoog Scout Reservation tolls each noon for them. The ringing of the bell is a Yawgoog tradition and the bell is rung to this day. While some Scouts and former Scouts went to war, the Scouts at home (2,000 strong) enrolled in Messengers for Civilian Defense. They collected 11,480,643 pounds of wastepaper; picked up 144,000 pounds of aluminum; tackled two State-wide house to house distributions of war time instruction, distributing 200,000 copies in each project; distributed 150,000 war posters; solicited 30,780 books for servicemen; went to Aroostook County, Maine, for a month and picked 90,000 barrels of potatoes which otherwise would not have been harvested. A total of 7,195 war service ribbons each representing six complete war-time projects were awarded to Scouts and 540 boys and men received the coveted "War Service Ace" strip for outstanding help to their country.

Advancement was always a priority since the first Eagle Scout rank was granted in 1919 to James J. Deery, who went on to graduate from the United States Military Academy and become a colonel in the United States Army. In 1961, the increase in Scout membership, the large number of Eagle Candidates and the desire to recognize all the Eagles, led to the inception of the Eagle Scout Recognition Dinner, at which each boy is sponsored by a prominent person usually someone with a vocation in which the Eagle Scout is interested.

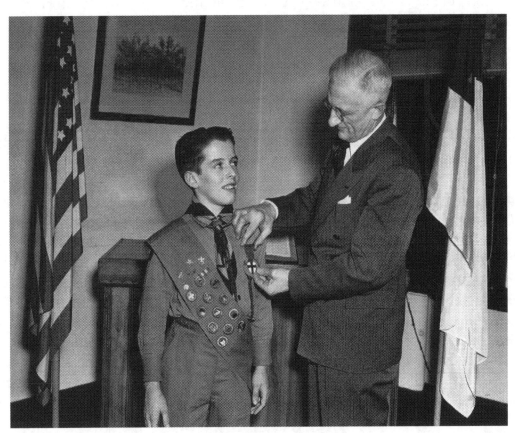

Rev. Earl Hollier Tomlin, Executive Secretary of the RI Council of Churches awarding the first God and Country recognition to Star Scout Elden G. Bucklin, Jr. on February 10th, 1946.

The post war years were years of great growth and development with the membership more than doubling from 12,000 to 26,000 at the end of 1962. They were years of forward steps in financing, in building up the professional staff, in improving administration techniques, in strengthening the Scouting Districts as operating groups and expanding camping sites and camping facilities. Great leadership certainly had an impact on the post war years. (See Scouting's Top Leaders at the end of this writing.) Paul C. Nicholson, Jr., President of Nicholson File, served as Council President in 1957 and 1958. While Paul was President, the Council moved its office from 26 Custom House Street to 51 Empire Street. He started the studies which resulted in the Golden Jubilee capital campaign for funds for the new Scout Center and the expansion of Yawgoog and he carried on as Chairman of the Scout Center Building Committee. The securing of the site at 175 Broad Street in Providence was one of his great accomplishments. Mr. Nicholson went on to serve as President of the Rhode Island Boy Scouts from 1969 to 1996.

William J. Gilbane, Executive Vice President of Gilbane Building Company, served as President during 1959 and 1960 during the preparations and celebrations of the Golden Jubilee Campaign. In 1962 and 1963 Aaron H. Roitman served as President of the Council overseeing the change of administration of Chief Williams to the election of H. Cushman Anthony as Deputy Scout Executive and the installation of Robert F. Parkinson as the new Scout Executive of the Narragansett Council. While Council Presidents served for a year or two, Council Treasurers held their titles for much longer.

The first Council Treasurer was Edward S. Moulton whose term lasted from 1919 thru 1950. He was followed by F. C. Pearce Drummond as Treasurer and then Donald C. Dewing in 1955 who served as Council Treasurer until 1986. Arthur R. Langlais took over as Council Treasurer in 1987 serving thru 1991. Mr. Dewing remained as Treasurer for the Rhode Island Boy Scouts until his death in December of 1988. Don Dewing also served as Scoutmaster of Troop 82 Providence from 1927 until his death in 1988. The two-year term as Council Treasurer was adopted in 1992 to coincide with the two-year term for Council President. John J. Schibler served as Council Treasurer in 1992 and 1993; Michael El-Hillow who was CFO at A.T. Cross Company was Council Treasurer in 1994 and 1995; Charles N. Coates served in 1996; and Donald W. Reilly served from 1997 thru 1998; Joseph P. Gencarella served from 1999 to 2001; Robert A. DiMuccio from 2002 thru 2005; Andrew C. Hewitt from 2006 thru 2009; and Barry F. Morrison is serving as Council Treasurer at the time of this writing.

There have been many benefactors to Scouting throughout the years but it would be impossible to name all of them. Below is just a brief look at some of them.

- Captain George Bucklin Trust Fund which erected the Bucklin Memorial Buildings at Yawgoog
- U.S. Senator and Mrs. Jesse H. Metcalf gave money for the development of the main camp's water-supply system, erection of many Adirondack Shelters and the stocking of Yawgoog Pond. In addition, in 1939 Mrs. Metcalf funded the Metcalf Lodge at Sandy Beach which was erected in memory of her husband.
- Mrs. Edward S. (Elizabeth Armington) Moulton donated the Armington Memorial Health Lodge at Yawgoog in 1941 in memory of her father, Col. James H. Armington.

- Albert E. Lownes gave his 250-acre estate, Aquapaug on Worden Pond in South Kingstown in 1955 for camping and for a wildlife and botanical sanctuary.
- A. Livingston Kelley bequeathed in 1956 his 225-acre woodland and waterfront area on Narrow River in North Kingstown as a camping reservation (called Kelgrant).
- Harry C. Curtis bequeathed in 1935 a sum of money used to purchase 150 acres of land adjoining the Yawgoog property which is known as Curtis Tract.
- The memory of George B. Champlin has been perpetuated at the Champlin Scout Reservation with gifts from Mr. & Mrs. George S. Champlin.
- Infantry Lodge, Inc., a group of infantry officers who served with Scout Commissioner Col. G. Edward Buxton, presented Scouting in 1950 with 30 acres of land and a one-story frame building in Rehoboth, Massachusetts, in memory of their former comrade and friend. The property is known as Camp Buxton.
- The Williams Amphitheatre at Yawgoog was initially constructed from money donated by Scouts and Scouters of the Council in 1943 and enlarged with a gift from the Champlins made to the Jubilee Fund.

The growth of Camp Yawgoog continues even today since the first week of camp in 1916 when tents were pitched in the field north of the Palmer farmhouse and cooking was over an outdoor army field range. In 1917 and 1918 the tents were in a company street in the field and apple orchard south of the house. In 1919, a well was drilled and a 'mess' hall and kitchen were erected beside the farmhouse which served as the camp office. The tents were pitched in a circle with the council fire in the center. As the attendance grew, Troop Camps Tuocs, Oak Ridge and Pioneer were cut out of the woods along the shore and the circle of tents became a group of troop camps.

As more and more Scouts attended camp, a survey was done in 1924 to solve the problem of how to increase the dining facilities. The survey plan called for divisions and in 1924 the second dining hall was built just back of the shore, first called Bucklin, then Three Point, then Sharpe Lodge. Yawgoog operated as two divisions, an "Upper Division" around the first dining hall and "Three Point Division" on the shore. The swimming beach at Three Point was cleared of rocks and in 1925 Phillips Island was purchased and an outpost camp was set up there. Trails were opened up through the property and a council ring and nature den was established. The Upper and Three Point Divisions became overcrowded and the beach was too small. Expansion was a must and the purchase of all the land around Yawgoog Pond was accomplished by T. Dawson Brown.

In 1929 the Medicine Bow Division was established and Rathom Lodge was built to take the place of the Upper Division and to increase its capacity. It had its own beach and its own activity area. The forest fire of 1930 restricted the use of the woods but brought about the creation of the Stockade for crafts and camping skills and the expansion of the canoeing, sailing and fishing programs and the building of Fort Hilton, a camping, trading and outfitting post on Hill 407 at the south end of Yawgoog Pond. It also started the reforestation and Forestry Corps programs which made Yawgoog green again.

BUCKLIN MEMORIAL BUILDING
CAMP YAWGOOG
ROCKVILLE, R.I.

In 1931, the Captain George Bucklin Buildings were dedicated on the site of the old Upper Division. This group of buildings included the great memorial lodge, the two cedar log cabins, the rebuilding of the first dining hall into a trading post, the gateway and the garage and equipment shed. To these buildings were later added the Ranger's House, the Workshop and Storage Building. The expansion of the property continued with the purchase of the cottages on Rocky Point and the acquisition of Curtis Tract, bringing the total Yawgoog acreage to 800.

The hurricane of 1938 was a disaster for Yawgoog but a saw mill rig was brought in and lumber was cut which was used in the erection of Metcalf Lodge and the creation of the Sandy Beach Division in 1939. The building of the Williams Amphitheatre, the three Worship Centers (St. John Bosco Chapel for Scouts of the Catholic faith, the Cathedral in the Woods for Protestant worship and the Temple of the Ten Commandments), and the Armington Memorial Health Lodge took place in the 1940's. In 1953, the water rights to Yawgoog and Wincheck Ponds were secured and it became possible to maintain a constant high level of water.

Clinton L. Armstrong was year-round ranger at Yawgoog from 1934 until his retirement in 1959 after 25 years of service. He designed and developed the War Memorial Bell Tower. A senior and junior honor society was developed at Yawgoog—the Knights of Yawgoog and the Wincheck Indians. In 1957, the Wincheck Indians became Wincheck Lodge, Order of the Arrow, a great national camping brotherhood. In 2001 when the Narragansett Council and the Moby Dick Council merged, the two Order of the Arrow Lodges merged as well and became known as the Abnaki Lodge. In 1961, $300,000 of the Golden Jubilee Fund was used to expand Yawgoog main camps to 1200-boy capacity, to reconstruct the three dining halls, to build fine new latrines and wash houses and redevelop the beaches and otherwise refurnish and re-equip the camps.

For many years Albertus M. Colvin of Cranston had permitted the Council to use his "Skeleton Valley' property in Cranston. In 1949, money was provided from a family foundation for the purchase of 100 acres of land on Joy Brook at Dugway Hill, Scituate Avenue in Cranston. In the years following, this foundation gave money anonymously for the creation of a Ranger's House, shelters, ponds, roads, wells, headquarters, security fencing and many other developments, as well as the addition of 32 more acres of land and the maintenance of a resident Camp Ranger. In 1954 the donors gave permission to name the property, "The George B. Champlin Reservation". Champlin Scout Reservation has become one of the most useful and most used assets of the Narragansett Council serving as a training center, Cub Scout Day Camp, as well as many other events.

Narragansett Council now operates two Scout Shops/Service Centers (one in the Summit Square Plaza on Route 2 in Warwick, RI and one across from the Swansea Mall in Swansea, MA) and owns and operates eight camps: Camp Aquapaug in South Kingstown, Buck Hill Scout Reservation and Cub World in Burrillville, Camp Buxton in Rehoboth, Mass., Cachalot Scout Reservation in Plymouth, Mass., Champlin Scout Reservation in Cranston, Sandsland on Block Island and Yawgoog Scout Reservation in Rockville. Administrative functions are housed at 10 Risho Avenue in East Providence.

AN ADDRESS BY COL. BUXTON
Taken from: "25 Years of Scouting in Rhode Island"

1910 to 1935

Twenty-five years ago two young lawyers met on the northwest corner of Westminster and Dorrance Streets. They had been close friends through several years of association in the Rhode Island National Guard. One was thirty-four years old—the other was twenty-nine.

The older man was tall, straight—a soldier from the top of his red head to his heels. He spoke with great animation and serious purpose; but from time to time his face lit up with an unusual smiling charm and humorous crinkles around his eyes. He was a natural leader because he used his imagination and optimism and courage to help other people and very rarely thought of himself. His life has reminded me of one of the early figures of the Roman Republic, like Cincinnatus. He had the love for his City and State which motivated Horatius. He shared the ideals of citizenship expressed by Cato and Cicero and Horace and Virgil. He also had a genius for friendship. He spent his life working for his City and State, and he died in the service of the Federal Government. His name was Charles E. Mulhearn and there is a square in Providence which memorializes his spirit and his service.

The younger of the two, who met on the street corner that day, a quarter of a century ago, was I.

"Have you been reading about General Baden-Powell and his Scout movement for boys?" said Mulhearn. His interest had been caught by press notices and the further announcement that an organization called the "American Boy Scouts" was developing in Boston, under the leadership of the *Boston American*. Colonel Mulhearn had visited their headquarters and obtained a copy of Baden-Powell's first Manual.

He gave me a copy to read and said that if I was interested in inaugurating such a movement in Rhode Island with him, he would be willing to "take off his hat and coat," as he put it, and "go to work". I went home and read the manual from cover to cover, met the Colonel the next day and we pledged ourselves to this task.

Neither of us liked the idea of accepting the leadership of the American Boy Scouts, but since no other organization in America was formally incorporated, we felt it would be necessary to affiliate for the time being, in order to get the benefit of existing experience, and contact with the English movement. We had neither money, backers, headquarters nor followers.

The records of the organization show that on September 6, 1910, a meeting was held in the office of the General Treasurer, Walter A. Read, at the State House. Colonel Mulhearn was elected Chief Scout of the State. Other officers elected were: Secretary, Judge Howard B. Gorham; Treasurer, Mr. Read; County Commissioners, G. Edward Buxton, Jr., for Providence, Rowland G. Hazard for Washington County.

The next step in organization was a meeting called by me as Scout Commissioner of Providence County, in the old Talma Theatre, on October 6, 1910. We had secured the following Committee for Providence County who joined in supporting the call for the meeting: Ex-Governor James H. Higgins, Colonel Frank W. Matteson, Colonel Harry Cutler, Walter Callender and Antonio A. Capotosto.

I called the meeting to order and State Treasurer Walter A. Read was elected to preside over the meeting, with Captain Everitte S. Chaffee as Secretary. It is my recollection that there were about one hundred and fifty citizens present. Colonel Mulhearn made an enthusiastic report of progress which had been achieved in the past month, stating that five troops had been formed and announced the names of the three County Scout Commissioners, Adjutant General Charles W. Abbot, Jr., having been appointed for Bristol County.

The newspaper account states that Superintendent of Schools Randall J. Condon announced that the use of any school room in the city would be extended for Scout purposes and Harry Cutler, Treasurer of the County organization, announced that pledges had been obtained for approximately $1,000.00 to further the expenses of organization work. The only salary proposed was for a stenographer in headquarters.

I recall that Mr. Frederick Roy Martin then Editor of the Journal, surprised us at this meeting by announcing that his corporation would furnish headquarters for the Scout movement, rent free, for so long a period as we wished to avail ourselves of such facilities.

You will be interested to know that the same newspaper account includes among those who attended and spoke in support of the movement the name of James A. Williams, who little dreamed at the time that his 12-year old son would eventually become one of Rhode Island's most useful citizens—the Scout Executive and central personality of Scouting, as well as a conspicuous figure in the development of a great national movement.

It is significant in a state founded by Roger Williams, upon the conception of complete religious liberty and freedom of conscience, that from the outset, this movement was give the hearty approval of all denominations and sects, and that no religious group desired to limit to itself the benefits of Scouting. Among the many clergymen who supported our efforts on the basis of undivided citizenship and Americanism, I recall with grateful appreciation the Most Reverend James Dewolf Perry, Monsignor Peter E. Blessing, Rabbi Samuel Gup, and Dr. William H. P. Faunce.

By October 24, 1910, headquarters had been opened in Room 14 of the Journal Building, and Providence County had five troops.

At the beginning, Colonel Mulhearn and I jointly attended the ceremonies connected with the formation of these troops, but as the movement grew, we found it necessary to divide our time and alternate our responsibilities. I have always remembered the day on which I formed the Third Providence Troop in the Slater Avenue School and I take a pardonable satisfaction in the recollection that I administered the oath and gave preliminary instructions to an enthusiastic and bright-eyed youngster named Harold Williams.

It is impossible to reminisce in anything but the most sketchy fashion concerning the incidents and the personalities of those early years. Many of those leaders have received an honorable discharge from the Scouting of this world. It is easy to believe that their vivid personalities and boundless energies are engaged in the promotion of citizenship and the common welfare in other camping grounds, bordering on unknown rivers and boundless seas.

There was a lot of fun in those early days. Judge Capotosto will remember the thrills and merriment of the episode in which he and I aided Commissioner Rathom in a brilliant night attack upon the Judge's troop as it lay dreaming at its fireside in the gloomy wood to be awakened by ferocious and savage cries, terrorized by the crashing of John Rathom's two hundred and sixty-nine pounds in the nearby brush.

This movement owes much, in its formative days, to the personalities of John Rathom, Harry Cutler and T.F. I. McDonnell. They were busy men. They had many responsibilities in the world of public affairs and business. But nothing in their busy lives assumed the importance of, or took precedence over, all other interests as did the Rhode Island Boy Scouts. These men had a vision of the future Republic, strengthened by sound bodies and healthy brains, supported by standards of self-discipline and a lively sense of citizenship, which epitomizes the spirit of Scouting.

The great problem of Scoutmasters arose, and we were fortunate indeed in finding young men like T. Dawson Brown, Milton MacIntosh, Herbert Dean, Captain John England, Prescott Lovell, Harold Babcock, Bob Thackeray, Grafton Kenyon, Ben Utter, George Fish, John Chafee and others on that honorable roster who were willing to learn patiently, by trial and error, the technique of boy leadership, on a scale never before attempted.

It will be remembered that for a period of years, the Rhode Island Boy Scouts continued an independent existence from the Boy Scouts of America, although the latter had troops in both Newport and the Blackstone Valley. It was not our intention to be stubbornly provincial in our hesitation to merge our identity with what had become a national movement, although our action may be said to have reflected some typical Rhode Island characteristics. You will remember that our State, although the first to strike a blow in the Revolutionary War, was the last to assent to the formation of the Federal Government. A small, compact geographical unit is perhaps more likely to assert its individualistic identity than a larger territory, which possesses a greater sense of security.

However, this movement meant so much to those of us who had created it that we waited a while to be sure that the heads of the national organization were actuated by similar purposes—that the good of the boy was being placed first and that leadership was not inspired by either a hope of personal aggrandizement or a love of power. It may be that we were strengthened in our determination to go alone through some formative years by the far-sighted philanthropy of Captain Bucklin, whose generosity enabled us to finance our State-wide organization and to build up that great laboratory experiment in troop camping, Camp Yawgoog.

Suffice to say that in early 1917 a meeting took place in our headquarters between half a dozen of our Rhode Island leaders and the Chief Scout Executive of the Boy Scouts of America. After a few preliminary clashes of personality, we found we were speaking the same language and without further hesitation threw in our lot with that great national body.

Since those first days, which we celebrate tonight, the years have thundered past. The first Rhode Island Scouts are men of forty. Upon their competent shoulders have, these many years, rested the burdens and privileges of manhood, in peace and in war. Some of them fought through the Valley of the Aire and the Hindenberg Line, in our wartime regiments. Some died, with their young American comrades, that another generation might grow in usefulness and dignity through at least an interval of peace and security.

I do not know or care much what will be the economic order of tomorrow, if the Boy Scouts of America determine the quality of our future men. Our civilization will be assured. Out of this small experiment in citizenship and in the art of living has sprung a mighty force, which shall bind in ties of brotherhood the races which have inherited our continent.

Wave after wave of Scouts will advance and the arena of modern American life will be a better place for the weak and the strong alike because you leaders have imparted your vision of truth and courage and resourcefulness and unselfishness; because you have demonstrated that the forces of Nature are friendly to the trained man; because you preached the value of co-operative action and self-respect; because you have fostered by word and example a sense of pride in the obligations of citizenship, far more potent than the fear of the guard-house.

You have asked me tonight to talk a while about our beginnings and some of the early leaders. I feel the inadequacy of my remarks. One would wish to say much of the experiments, aspiring failures, and human accomplishment of a twenty-five year saga in the lives of thousands of men and boys. I should have liked to pay tribute to the subsequent leaders of Rhode Island Scouting. The roster of their names is written in the hearts of those they served. They belong to the only aristocracy that matters—those who demand much of themselves.

I charge you to accept your larger role and your greater destiny under the splendid leadership of your present Scout Executive. No man more justifies his entrance upon the stage of manhood than do you in the parts you play. And none will win to larger rewards than you receive in what you do.

May I close with one word which I utter without reservation, on behalf of the Rhode Island founders, no longer here. You have built far beyond their dream. You have justified their deepest faith. I seem to hear the living spirit of Scouting speaking to each of us through those lines of Rudyard Kipling:

> *"Also we will make promise. So long as the Blood endures,*
> *I shall know that your good is mine. Ye shall feel that my strength is yours:*
> *In the day of Armageddon, at the last great fight of all*
> *That our House stand together, and the pillars do not fall."*

HIGH TIDES IN RHODE ISLAND SCOUTING
A BRIEF HISTORY BY SCOUT EXECUTIVE J. HAROLD WILLIAMS

1910-1935

It threw together, on a Providence street corner early in the summer, two young men who liked boys, Colonel Charles E. Mulhearn, 34 years old, and Captain G. Edward Buxton, Jr., 29 years old—and started a conversation which resulted in the formation of the Scout organization in the State.

It swept into the heart of that great personality, John R. Rathom, editor of the Providence Journal, and captured his glowing interest and enthusiasm which gave Scouting its driving force and character during its early years.

In September, 1910, the first sponsoring organization was formed and the Washington Park unit was recognized as the First Providence Troop with a membership of 64 Scouts and with Herbert R. Dean, a young cavalryman, as the first Scoutmaster in the State. That was 25 years ago.

1935—Looking Back at the First 25 Years

On January 8, 1935, at the 25th annual meeting of the Narragansett Council, Boy Scouts of America, 231 troops with 5,479 Scouts and an adult membership of 1,615 were recognized. In addition, there were 13 Cub Packs with a membership of 244 Cubs and 60 Cub leaders.

In 1910, Scouting in Rhode Island was an idea. In 1935, it was a reality—with a great and steadily growing membership, a magnificent camping reservation at Yawgoog, scores of district and troop hiking sites, a successful leadership training program, complete district organization, the Jamboree recognized as the greatest show in the State, a loyal and enthusiastic corps of leadership of increasingly "higher type", and a National reputation.

In these first 25 years, troops graduated approximately 25,000 boys from the ranks of Scouting into the ranks of citizenship. Hundreds of these boys would personally testify to the value of Scouting in their lives. Who knows what it had done for others—what leisure-time happiness it had created, what characters it had molded, or what lives it had saved?

During these 25 years, death had taken many of Scouting's staunch supporters—Colonel Mulhearn, John Rathom, Adjutant General Abbot, Harry Cutler, Walter Read, Frank B. McSoley, Arthur L. Lake, George L. Gross, George Bucklin, Walter Hidden and Dr. Charles Hitchcock. T.F.I. McDonnell had been ill and confined to his home for a long time.

Others who had been active though the years by this time were now out of active service but still gave Scouting continued interest and support, including Colonel Buxton, N. Stuart Campbell, George B. Utter, William B. MacColl, Judge Howard B. Gorham, Judge A. A. Capotosto, Grafton I. Kenyon, Richard S. Aldrich, E. S. Chaffee, Donald S. Babcock, Carl B. Marshall, Dr. Dennett L. Richardson, G. Maurice Congdon, E. S. Hartwell, Robert Johnston and Andrew Meiklejohn.

Others would carry on for years to come—Donald North, T. Dawson Brown, Edward S. Moulton, Professor Fred W. Marvel, Wilbur A. Scott, and a host of younger men with the same faith and enthusiasm in boyhood.

A Personal Touch

Scout Executive J. Harold Williams, the author of "25 Years of Scouting in Rhode Island" from which these historical excerpts were taken, was one of the first Scouts to join in September 1910 and it was "the great privilege of his life" to have grown up with Scouting in Rhode Island and with the personalities which had made it.

The following paragraphs are a brief historical sketch that he thought would be more pleasing to the reader if "written in reminiscent and personal style".

"My father brought home one night a red-covered book, Scouting for Boys by Lieut. General Sir Robert Baden-Powell, and laid it on the table. "Son," he said, "you might read this and see what you think of it."

By the next morning, I had gone through it as only a 12-year-old can devour a book. "Dad," I said, "I want to be one."

"You form a patrol," father explained, "and then report to Colonel Charles E. Mulhearn, the probation officer."

At school, the Owl patrol was organized, and Joe Cummings, as patrol leader, and I, as assistant, found ourselves knocking at Colonel Mulhearn's office door next Saturday morning "to report".

We were scared. A colonel is a colonel and a probation officer is a probation officer. Charles E. Mulhearn, however, was a man. He rose, shook hands with us, told us he was our friend, and treated us like men. From that day on, he was one of my heroes.

Col. Mulhearn assigned the Owls to the Third Providence Troop, forming at Slater Avenue School with Prescott W. Lovell as Scoutmaster, and on the next Saturday, we marched into the school yard and reported. That morning, I met my second great Scout hero, whose luster never faded, G. Edward Buxton, Jr. He invested the troop and initiated us into the first mysteries of Scoutcraft."

Stories of John R. Rathom

Mr. Rathom was a gigantic man, physically as well as in other ways. When his associates finally persuaded him to get a uniform, he couldn't get into the trousers until his tailor inserted a large "V" in the seat. This "V" was always an organization joke.

Mr. Rathom used to tell a story on himself about forming a troop in Wanskuck. During the organization meeting, Mr. Rathom gave the youngsters a talk on the evils of smoking. He told them that no growing boy ought to smoke and drove the point home by telling them that the big African game hunters of his acquaintance did not smoke on safari in order to have steady aim when charged by wild beast.

"As I came out of the hall after the meeting," Mr. Rathom said, "there was a youngster smoking a cigarette. I asked him, 'Didn't you hear my speech?' 'Sure', he replied. 'Well, why are you smoking?' I asked. The boy looked at me in disgust; 'Hell, mister, there ain't no lions in Wanskuck.'"

He was a real personality to all us Scouts. I was fortunate enough to get to know him personally when I was picked to take a leading part in the Scout Minstrel Show at the old Opera House on February 5-6, 1912. Mr. Rathom had written a very funny parody on Mark Antony's oration over Caesar's body and I used to go down to his office after school to rehearse it.

The show was a great success. At the time "Alexander's Rag Time Band" was all the rage. On the way to the theater for the second show, Mr. Rathom heard a hurdy gurdy playing the tune. I remember his calling Scoutmaster Arthur Lake to him backstage: "Lake, I want that hurdy gurdy on stage. Go and get it. I don't know where it is, but go and get it. Don't argue. Get out." Mr. Lake got the hurdy gurdy.

One could go on for hours telling John R. Rathom stories—about his visits to troops, his battles, his trips to the camps with Capt. Jack Crawford and many other characters, his appearances at rallies in an old hat with a line of fish hooks caught into the band.

J. R.'s Last Message

J. Harold Williams continued. "May I tell just one more? It was September 25, 1923. Mr. Rathom was in his last illness, abed to his cabin at Kennebago Lake, Maine. I had become Scout Executive of the organization, and was at Kennebago with other New England executives for a conference. Three of us, Roy Berry of Boston, Don North and I went in to see Mr. Rathom just as the sun was setting over Spotted Mountain.

His great form had wasted away. We asked him if he read much.

"No, I can't read," he said, "but I can remember most every novel I ever read—characters, action, even some dialogue. Today, I have been going through the *Tale of Two Cities*. It's easy reading. It saves your eyes."

Then he gave us his last message to Scouting: *"The American boy—that complicated bundle of contradictions—is the greatest and most wonderful experimental laboratory on earth, and he can be made either the hope or the despair of the world. It is to the former goal that the efforts of the Boy Scouts of America are pledged; and as long as our people still hold to the basic virtues the work cannot fail. God speed every activity in that direction."*

The Boy Scouts of America

Outside Rhode Island, the American Boy Scout organization was out of existence, and the Boy Scouts of America, chartered in the District of Columbia on February 8th, 1910, was becoming the great National Scout organization.

Newport and Pawtucket had never become affiliated with the Rhode Island Boy Scouts, although the Rhode Island Boy Scouts had organized one Boy Scout troop in Pawtucket, with Stewart Little as Scoutmaster in May 1911, which lasted a short while.

In Newport, Ernest Thompson Seton, Chief Scout of the Boy Scouts of America, lectured at the Y.M.C.A. in the summer of 1910, and from this meeting an organization developed which resulted in a committee meeting on January 8, 1911, at the home of Mrs. Nicholas Brown, with some 25 persons interested in Scouting present. In February, 1911, the Newport Council was organized at the office of Superintendent of Schools Lull. Among those present were: Major Lorillard Spencer of New York, Austin T. Sands, Capt. W. McCarthy Little, Commander P. W. Hourigan, H. W. N. Powell, Stephen P. Cabot, Wilfred H. Chapin, D. Leroy Dresser, Walter A. Wright, A. R. C. Gatzenmeier, Henry S. Hendy and Mr. Lull.

Harold Warden's original patrol had grown into Troop 1 Newport, with Austin L. Sands as Scoutmaster. Mr. Gatzenmeier became a Scoutmaster in February, 1911, and also became the first Scout Commissioner for Newport.

Until 1920, Newport was a second class council with Mr. Gatzenmeier as Commissioner. In that year, a first class council was organized with Robert E. Gurley as Scout Executive. He was followed, after two years of service, by Lawrence K. Ebbs, who held office for one year.

Newport then became a second class council again without an Executive until 1929 when it merged with the State organization and became the Newport Area of Narragansett Council.

Scouting in Blackstone Valley

The first Boy Scouts of America troops were started in Blackstone Valley in 1911. A unit in the First Baptist Church in Pawtucket was recognized as Troop 1, Pawtucket, with Albert L. Copeland as Scoutmaster. Troop 2, Pawtucket, was organized by the Bethany Free Baptist Church with Thomas A. Holt as Scoutmaster.

Andrew Meiklejohn and Robert Johnson were instrumental in the organization of the Pawtucket-Central Falls Council, Boy Scouts of America, in 1916, and Mr. Meiklejohn became first President. The Scout Executives of Pawtucket included: John D. McEwen, 1917-1918; Charles A. Holmes, 1919-1920; George W. Fairchild, 1920; William Lee Abbot, 1922-1930.

The Council operated a camp at Quonset Point in 1918; Camp Sterling near Hope in 1919 and 1920; at Norton in 1922; and Camp Hill on Flat River Reservoir in Coventry from 1923 to 1930.

At the time of the merger of the Pawtucket-Central Falls Council with the Narragansett Council in the fall of 1930, the former's territory included Pawtucket, Central Falls, Lincoln and Cumberland, with a membership of approximately 20 troops.

The Woonsocket Council was organized in 1924 with John C. Cosseboom as President, and Arthur S. Gemme as Scout Executive, who was followed by James B. Dodds. Mr. Dodds was Executive at the time of the merger of Woonsocket Council with the Narragansett Council in the fall of 1930.

One of the big accomplishments of the Woonsocket group was the Acquisition of a 125 acre camp-site on Wakefield Pond. This camp, which was named Winnesuket, was purchased by the Kiwanis Club of Woonsocket and deeded to three trustees who leased it to the Woonsocket Scouts.

Boys' Life Starts Here—Kind of!

Boys' Life, now the official Boy Scout magazine, got its start in Rhode Island in 1911. At least this is what is reported by J. Harold Williams in his *Scout Trails 1910-1962, The Story of Scouting in Rhode Island*. J. Harold notes that 18 year old RI Boy Scout, Joseph Lane, labeled and founded *Boys' Life* as the "Official Boy Scout Magazine" in 1911. Williams reported that Providence businessman, Edward M. Fay provided Lane moral and financial support for his venture. Williams stated that *Boys' Life* was purchased by the BSA on July 19, 1912. Williams literally lived through this time period, knew Lane and Fay personally and recounted a 1959 reunion meeting with Lane and Fay where he listened to their stories about the early 'shoestring' days of *Boys Life*. Williams had nothing to gain and as a man of consummate honesty, whether Lane was the founder of *Boys' Life* or an Editor on Barton's staff would probably make little difference. Dr. John T. Dizer, professor and dean emeritus of Mohawk Valley Community College in Utica, New York, Silver Beaver Scouter joined the BSA as a boy in 1933 and has made a study of boys' books for 25 years. Professor Dizer, on the other hand, credits George S. Barton of Somerville, MA, as founder, publisher and first editor of *Boys' Life*. As most Scouters know, 1910 marked the official beginning of the Boy Scouts of America but many do not know that the American Boy Scouts and the New England Boy Scouts were also formed that year. Dizer reports that in 1910, George S. Barton was in his 30's, an official with the American Boy Scouts, which was sponsored by the California newspaper mogul, William Randolph Hearst. In December, however, citing financial irregularities in the group, Hearst withdrew his support. A cadre from the ABS's New England Division also abandoned ship at that time and formed the New England Boy Scouts. Barton, Edwin Randolph Short and E. W. Gay became officials of the New England organization. All three helped staff *Boys' Life*: Barton as editor, Short as assistant editor and Gay as circulation manager. In March of 2011, Barton hired Joseph J. Lane, an 18 year old Scout from Rhode Island, as advertising manager and assistant editor. The first issue was published in Boston in January but once Barton added to his staff and worked on changes the second issued appeared on March 1, 1911. This issue was often incorrectly identified as the first but because Barton drastically changed the format and the size of the magazine, he labeled the March issue as "Vol. 1, No. 1". Later the magazine moved to Providence when financial support was furnished by Edward M. Fay. On July 19, 1912, it was purchased by the Boy Scouts of America to become one of the leading publications of the country. Since all the original players are long gone, it's a matter of who believes what. You decide!

The Boy Scouts of America urged the Rhode Island Boy Scouts to merge, and much correspondence was exchanged and many conferences held. Mr. Rathom and his associates felt that the national organization was too cumbersome, too sectarian, and that it was not making an appeal to all classes of boys.

But both organizations tempered their views and methods. Congress chartered the Boy Scouts of America on June 15th 1916. The approach of the World War was bringing the national organization governmental recognition and in May, 1917, the Rhode Island Boy Scouts voted to merge with the Boy Scouts of America. The Rhode Island Boy Scouts retained its corporate identity, but the operating body became known as the Greater Providence Council, Boy Scouts of America. The National Organization was given the right to organize other councils in Newport, Pawtucket, and Woonsocket.

Leaders of '12, '13, '14, and '15

But to go back again, Adjutant General Abbot was succeeded by Col. Harry Cutler as Chief Scout for 1912 and 1913. His speeches condemning racial prejudices and extolling patriotism are not to be forgotten.

The next Chief Scout, in 1914, was Frank B. McSoley, an efficient young engineer and early wireless expert who had made a mark as a Scoutmaster. He was Scouting's Beau Brummel and made a grand figure in uniform—field glasses and all.

Arthur L. Lake, the popular Court House Superintendent and North Providence Scoutmaster, was Chief Scout in 1915. He was a very stout man, and Williams never forgot the fall on the ice he took outside the door of his troop meeting place. It broke up the troop meeting. But Arthur Lake never stood on dignity. He was a real friend to everyone.

In South Kingstown, Grafton I. Kenyon was Scoutmaster of a very large and flourishing unit, formed in 1911.

Scouting was going now in Warwick, where it had been organized in 1911 by Edward L. Waterman; in Bristol, started in 1912 with George R. Fish as Scoutmaster; and in Westerly where it had been inaugurated in 1913 by George B. Utter, Robert G. Thackeray and Silas T. Nye.

Scouting Loses Ground

The organization had been losing ground during 1914 and 1915. The first wave of enthusiasm both on the part of the boys and men was wearing off. Leadership training efforts were inadequate. The lack of a printed manual was felt, although a second and first class badge had been designed and made available in 1914. Funds were scarce.

The volunteers directing the State and county organizations found it hard to give the time needed to keep troops going; to recruit leaders, to replace those resigning, to form new troops. John I. Rancourt had been employed as Assistant Commissioner to take charge of the headquarters in 1911, followed by John E. England who served from 1912 to 1916. Their work, however, was more secretarial than executive.

Only one troop formed in 1910 continued for the first 25 years without a breakdown and a period of inactivity. That troop was the First Providence Troop, and one of its traditions was that the troop never missed a meeting.

In January 1914, T. Dawson Brown organized the Second East Providence Troop and began his outstanding Scouting career. In March 1915, J. Harold Williams became a Scoutmaster and reorganized his old troop, the Third Providence.

By the first of 1916, the membership, which in 1912 had probably reached about 1,400, had fallen to approximately 500. There was bickering among Scoutmasters and but few activities. Affairs had reached a crisis. The Advisory Committee acted and Col. Buxton was chairman of the committee which brought to Rhode Island from Springfield, Donald C. North as the first real paid executive of the organization.

The First Executive Officer

Mr. North, who had been in Boys' Club work and probation work in the Massachusetts city, took up his duties early in 1916 with the title of Chief Scout. Of course, all the "independent" Rhode Island Scoutmasters resented an outsider's coming in "to boss us".

But Don North shortly won them over. He had two methods. One was to invite volunteers out to a beefsteak supper and the other was selling himself. His winning personality, his "line of jolly" and his sense of appreciation made them all "North Boosters" in a month or two.

Things began to boom again. Don North was a promoter. The organization raised some money. A little manual was printed. Scoutmasters' lectures were arranged. Don made speeches and gallivanted around the State from Narragansett to Woonsocket. He started the Boy Scout column in the *Sunday Journal.*

His greatest contribution was the fixing of our camping reservation at Yawgoog. He sold the organization the need for a permanent campsite, and then proceeded to find it. He visited about every lake or pond in the State and two sites were especially favored, Larkin's Pond and Yawgoog Pond. Larkin's Pond was lined with reeds and surrounded by fields and groves without a rock. Yawgoog was lined with ledges and surrounded by forest and rocks. Larkin's was nice. Yawgoog was rugged. The Boy Scouts took Yawgoog. Later the Girl Scouts located at Larkin's.

Camp Yawgoog opened on June 24, 1916, on the old Palmer farm, leased from the heirs. That fall, purchase negotiations were begun and by December, the Rhode Island Boy Scouts owned 130 acres on the shore of Yawgoog Pond.

The Chief Scout was busy. He had all the old-timers working and was bringing in new blood. New troops were forming in the fall. A rally and convention were held. The numbers began to increase again.

Then Came the War and Merger with the B.S.A.

Then came the war in 1917, followed by the merger with the Boy Scouts of America on May 22, 1917. They all became Boy Scouts of America in the Greater Providence

Council. T. F. I. McDonnell was elected President. Don North became Scout Executive. They changed their badges and plunged into war service.

They had mobilizations and patrolled beaches. Scouts planted corn and sold Liberty Bonds and War Savings Stamps, collected funds for the Red Cross, gathered fruit pits and tin foil, located black walnuts, raised flags, secured food conservation pledges, suspected spies, and performed a hundred and one other "back home" war services.

In the Second Liberty Loan, the Boy Scouts sold $399,700 in bonds; the Third, $452,550; and in the Fourth, $404,950. Scouts also sold $12,963 worth of War Savings Stamps.

The organization lost many Scoutmasters who went into service, and the Scout Executive had his hands full filling vacancies. But he bolstered up the morale with a big conference the last of 1917 by bringing to Rhode Island all the "big Bugs" from National Headquarters—Chief Scout Executive James E. West, National Scout Commissioner Daniel Carter Beard, Director of Education Lorne W. Barclay, "Pine Tee" James A. Wilder, Chief Sea Scout, and Chief Scout Librarian Franklin K. Mathiews—an array of national Scout talent never since equaled here. The membership in 1917 reached over 2000.

Under the leadership of Mr. McDonnell, Mr. North and others, plans were laid the first of 1918 for a big financial campaign for $40,000 to cover a three-year budget, and George L. Gross was secured as campaign chairman. In March, the drive was held and more than $52,000 was raised.

In February, Mr. North resigned to become Superintendent of Sockanosset School and was succeeded as Scout Executive by Raymond W. Seamans of Providence, who held office until the fall of 1918.

Our Benefactor, Captain George Bucklin

Capt. George Bucklin, a Civil War veteran, was the greatest benefactor of Rhode Island Scouting at that time. A native Rhode Islander, Capt. Bucklin had spent much of his life in the West. In the early days of Scouting in Providence, some unknown Scout performed Capt. Bucklin a service. The boy refused a tip as a good Scout should, and this captured the veteran's interest. He talked with John Rathom about Scouting and learned about its aims and purposes.

Capt. Bucklin died on August 25, 1918, and bequeathed a large sum of money in trust for the Rhode Island Boy Scouts, part of which was to be used in the erection of a memorial building. This fund made possible the purchase of 550 acres of the great

Yawgoog reservation, the building of the magnificent Bucklin Memorial Buildings at Yawgoog as a year-round camping and training center, and the carrying on of "our work".

There is a tablet at Yawgoog which says: "Scouts, When Passing This Spot, Salute the Memory of Capt. George Bucklin." We *do* salute him.

Captain George Bucklin
Born 1843
Died 1918 at the age of 75 in Long Beach, CA

A New Scout Executive

In December, 1918, the vacancy in the Scout Executive's office was filled by a partnership. J. Harold Williams was elected Acting Scout Executive to share the work of the position with Deputy Scout Commissioner T. Pitman Greene, a Spanish War veteran who was a very active and successful Scout leader. This arrangement lasted until the fall of 1919 when Mr. Williams was made the Scout Executive, which position he held until 1962.

A survey of active Scout membership at the beginning of 1919 revealed that the Scout enrollment had dropped to approximately 1,000. An intensive program of activities was developed and the work of the Court of Honor promoted with many Scouts earning merit badges, until March, 1919, James J. Deery of Troop 15 Providence, became the Council's first Eagle Scout. Deery later became an officer in the regular army. The Scouts turned out en masse to welcome the soldiers home in May, 1919, and in June, 1,200 Scouts paraded through the streets of Providence and held a rally at Brown University as a public demonstration. New troops began to form and enrollment was again on the upgrade.

From 1919 to 1935, membership grew from 1,000 to 5,500 Scouts and were very personal years to J. Harold Williams who stated that these years were "marked with the happiest kind of associations with loyal and inspired workers."

J. Harold 'Chief' Williams

Council Leadership from 1919 to 1935

T. F. I. McDonnell was President when J. Harold Williams took office. He had been one of the incorporators of the Rhode Island Boy Scouts and had been Treasurer and an active worker before he became President in 1917. He continued as head of the organization through 1921, and as an active member of the Board until his poor health restricted his activities. His interest in the development of Scouting was very keen.

Mr. McDonnell's charming personality and his friendship meant much to Williams as a 21-year-old executive and he always had the greatest affection for him. His enthusiasm as a public speaker and his vigor as a worker in the community life of Providence were of the greatest value to Scouting.

George L. Gross, as Chairman of the Board of Directors in 1918 and 1919, gave the Council a sound business administration. N. Stuart Campbell, another incorporator, served as Chairman of the Board in 1920-1921 and when that office was abolished by a complete revision of the by-laws, became President in 1922. To him the Council owes "our sound financial footing."

William B. MacColl, as President during 1923-1926, threw his vigorous personality into the work and was instrumental in the development of the intermediate district organizations which were so badly needed in a great organization covering most of the state.

T. Dawson Brown, who started as a Scoutmaster in 1914 and who had served as Council Secretary and Chairman of the most important Council Committees, became President in 1927, and held office until 1932. His was a most vigorous administration, perhaps the most vigorous and most noteworthy. During his term, the Jamboree, that great Scout circus at the Auditorium, was inaugurated, and the purchase of all the land surrounding Yawgoog Pond was accomplished.

The finest achievement was the bringing together, in one fine State organization, of the Newport, Blackstone Valley, Woonsocket and Greater Providence Councils, under the name of Narragansett Council. It was Mr. Brown who guided these mergers in 1929 and 1930 and who worked out the plan of Council operations.

It must be noted also that when Mr. Brown's term as President was finished, he went back to the most important job he could find in Scouting, that of being a Scoutmaster.

F. C. Pearce Drummond, another Scoutmaster grown up into Council leadership, then became President.

The following men served as Scout Commissioners during these 16 years: Col. Buxton, Col. Everitte S. Chaffee, Donald S. Babcock, Prof. William G. Vinal of the College of Education, who became an Eagle Scout to show boys the way, Mr. Drummond, Albert E. Lownes and then Donald North.

Edward S. Moulton came into Scouting in 1918 to audit the books and remained in that position until 1938. He was labeled a "devoted and efficient Treasurer, always more interested in the boys than in just keeping books." Moulton is credited with originating "that delightful Rhode Island Scouting event—the annual Squantum dinner to the Scoutmasters" which began in 1923.

Yawgoog

Professor Fred W. Marvel came into camp during the summer of 1919 as a visitor and was so impressed with the activities and discipline of the camp that he became a "Scout bug". In 1920, he became Chairman of the Camp Committee for 10 years. He preached the gospel of Yawgoog far and wide until he achieved the nickname of "the guy that owns Camp Yawgoog".

He saw Yawgoog grow in enrollment from 400 to 3,000 a season. He saw the building of Three Point Lodge and Rathom Lodge and the development of the camp from a mass unit to a series of divisions of troop camps, with all the attendant equipment and personnel.

It was a proud moment for him and for T. Dawson Brown when on July 8, 1928, in the presence of 1000 people, the 550 acres of Yawgoog pond and surrounding forestland were dedicated as a "Scout Adventureland Forever".

We should remember always the words of Col. Buxton that day as he made the dedication address:

"We dedicate these acres to the memory of the men who have made it possible. We dedicate this camp in recognition of the shy, yet deep, sense of duty which lies in the heart of the boy; we dedicate it to the spirit of greater understanding in future generations; and we dedicate it, finally, looking into the far distant future, to the time of a better, wiser and happier race."

The story of Yawgoog is not complete. Cushman Anthony and J. Harold Williams would never forget that Sunday afternoon of May 4, 1930, when the greatest forest fire in the history of Rhode Island swept down upon their beloved Yawgoog and devastated their glorious woods. They were there, powerless to stop it, and it laid its mark upon them and the forest.

How the loyal lovers of Yawgoog rallied there the next morning as the fire raged on; how a month later they set out 25,000 white pine seedlings among the charred stumps; how they came camping there just the same as nature strove to heal the wounds. These were warm memories to Williams.

In 1930, the Bucklin Fund trustees gave Council permission to erect the Bucklin Memorial at Yawgoog where it could be used by all the Scouts. G. Maurice Congdon was chairman of the building committee and F. Ellis Jackson the architect. Hours of meetings and conferences resulted in the development of that beautiful building with its gateway, garage, flanking cabins and pavilion which was dedicated on July 4, 1931, by Judge A. A. Capotosto, one of the charter members. The use of these buildings for year-round camping and leadership training went far beyond their dreams. In 1934, 2,400 scouts and leaders used them on weekends and vacation periods. They formed the heart of the Council.

The year 1930 also marked the acquisition of the 43-foot schooner Dolphin as a training ship for our Sea Scouts. This older boy division of Scouting was started in 1920 and has been a great value to older Scouts. In 1935, they were in the midst of a change of organization from that of independent Sea Scouts ships to that of Sea Scout Patrols and Divisions connected with troops in an effort to increase enrollment in the upcoming years, with the loyal support of Commodore Francis H. Stone, Jr.

At the same time, they were just beginning the development of Cubbing, "a junior Scout program for boys of 9, 10, and 11 years of age". In 1935, Narragansett Council had a Cub Scout enrollment of 244 "future Scouts".

Members of the Field Staff 1920-1935

The story would not be complete without mention of the men who were associated with Council's development during these years as Assistant and Field Executives. They were George R. Fish, 1919-1920; Eric P. Jackson, 1920-1921; Bradford H. Field, 1921-1925, and 1929-1935+*; Earle C. Beebe, 1921-1923; Nelson A. Sly, 1922-1926; Louis W. Gavitt, 1923-1928; Wilford S. Budlong, 1924; Christopher Gunderson, 1925-1933; Dana U. Lamb, 1926-1927; H. Cushman Anthony, 1927-1935+*, Arthur W. Leidman 1928-1935+*; Harold Silverman, 1930-1935+*, James B. Dodds, 1930-1934; C. Raymond Westcott, 1933-1935+*, Daniel W. Earle, 1934-1935+*.

Mr. Sly went on to become Scout Executive in Hartford, CT and Mr. Gunderson became S.E. in Cambridge, MA.

Narragansett Council, in 1935, was divided into areas and districts, each area being supervised by a paid officer, a Field Executive, and each district being in charge of a District Committee and a District Commissioner, volunteer workers. All of the members of the executive staff at that time came up through the ranks of the Council.

Mr. Anthony was the Executive for the Blackstone Valley Area, with headquarters at 33 Summer Street in Pawtucket. This area included the Daggett, Slater, Central Falls, and William Blackstone Districts.

Mr. Silverman and Mr. Westcott supervised the Providence Area with headquarters at 100 North Main Street, which included the North, East, South, West, Hope and Elmwood Districts.

Mr. Field was assigned to the Suburban Area, including Cranston, Woonasquatucket Valley, East Providence, Bristol County and Woonsocket Districts.

Mr. Leidman, in the Kent-South County Area, covered the West Shore, Pawtuxet Valley, Quequatuck and Narragansett Districts.

Mr. Earle was the Executive for the Newport Area, with headquarters at 179 Thames Street, Newport.

Clinton L. Armstrong was the Camp Warden for the Yawgoog reservation.

*1935+ has replaced the words "to the present" in section which was written in 1935.

Sixteen Years of Accomplishments

Williams reminisced about 1929-1935 as *"full of memories of rallies, meetings, civic service and associations with thousands of boys and men, but for myself, I am proudest of our steady growth, both in quantity and quality. We have developed active troop committees to help Scoutmasters where before there were only Scoutmasters working alone. We have developed active district committees and commissioners where before there were no intermediate organizations between the troop and the headquarters. We have developed a leadership training program, using the five Year Training Plan of the National Council, which is turning out trained leaders.*

We have helped in the development of the patrol system and boy leadership in our troops where before all was mass activity. We have seen a great advancement in outdoor craft and Scoutcraft technique, with 358 boys having reached the highest rank of Eagle Scout. We have seen our leadership being developed from the ranks. We are looking ahead to even greater numbers of Scouts in the years to come and to even better troops.

There is nothing else worth working for. Our work is only as effective as our troops. Our job is to form new troops and to help devoted Scoutmasters to conduct effective troops so that more and more boys—at least one out of every four—will be influenced by the spirit of Scouting.

I wish this brief sketch might contain the names of the wonderful Scoutmasters I have known, but space forbids and anyway, their names are engraved on the hearts of the boys they have guided.

Twenty-five years. It has been a long time and a short time. It has been work which has been fun.

We now turn our faces, our enthusiasm and our love for boys who soon will be men, toward the next 25 years which lie ahead."

From "25 Years of Scouting in Rhode Island, 1910-1935"
By J. Harold Williams
January 8, 1935

Gus Anthony and Charlotte Williams (Chief's wife)
remained friends until her death.

YAWGOOG FORESTRY CORPS

Following the Great Forest Fire of 1930, there was a need to plant and restore the forest in various areas of Camp. The Yawgoog Forestry Corps was formed in 1932 under the leadership of Clinton "Inkey" Armstrong, who would later go on to be the first resident Ranger at Yawgoog in 1933. The Forestry Corps operated each season until the start of World War II. Among the many tasks accomplished was the planting of more than 40,000 White Pine seedlings throughout Camp Yawgoog. The Medicine Bow area received a heavy concentration of seedlings. Many of these sturdy giants are still standing in the Bow. A walk from the Tim O'Neil Field down through Medicine Bow will reveal these beautiful pines lining both sides of Marvel Road.

An interesting side note to the early efforts of the Yawgoog Forestry Corps occurred in 1985 when Hurricane Gloria swept through Yawgoog and toppled a number of these large historical trees. The trees were harvested and brought to a local sawmill and cut into heavy planks. Throughout the years the lumber was used for a variety of special projects in camp. Squirreled away in the lumber rack by the Workshop and Storehouse were a number of thick, wide planks. These planks were taken out in 2003 and used to build the counters, shelves and tables in the 407 Outfitters (Trading Post) on the Donald North Court. Certainly this was a fitting use for this special White Pine. Although the planks are just part of one of these trees, careful counting of the annular rings will reveal the history of this lumber. Be sure to have a look.

The Yawgoog Forestry Corps was revived again in 1963 as part of Narragansett Council's successful effort to win the U.S. Department of Agriculture Council Conservation Award. Thirty-two Scouts along with a Scoutmaster, Assistant Scoutmaster, Junior Assistant Scoutmaster and a Quartermaster worked in this special program. They paid a reduced fee and spent part of their day doing forestry work and the other part engaged in all the activities Yawgoog has to offer. The forestry work consisted of thinning and pruning the many trees originally planted in the early thirties. They also supplied the firewood for the many sites in camp that no longer had dead wood available for camp fires. The 1963 Yawgoog Annual Report states, *"It was a happy, beneficial program for both boys and the camp."*

Forestry and conservation efforts continue today with many Scouts involved with a variety of projects. During the summer season, these efforts are coordinated by the Nature Center. Logging and tree planting occur in the off-season.

Year-by-Year Highlights of Narragansett Council History

1919 to 1962—J. Harold Williams, Scout Executive

Sea Scouting, the nautical branch of Scouting for older boys, got started in the early twenties in Rhode Island. Ships were organized in Warren, Bristol, Providence, Westerly, Newport, Pawtucket, Woonsocket, Warwick, and Riverside. Before World War II there were twenty-five ships and three hundred and fifty members registered, with cruises totaling 2,417 miles, annual regattas and ceremonial Bridges of Honor. During the years 1930 through 1935, Narragansett Council owned and operated the "Dolphin" a 43-foot Alden-built schooner. This beautiful ship had great appeal and gave wonderful seamanship training, but the limited number of boys who could be served each season and the high cost of operation forced the Council to sell her.

Chief J. Harold Williams pinning the Marvel Award on Paul J. Choquette, Jr. at Camp Yawgoog. The Marvel Award is given to the season's outstanding Scout at Yawgoog.

1953

The Rhode Island Boy Scouts purchased the Yawgo Line and Twine Company in 1953 for $40,000. The company (and therefore Rhode Island Boy Scouts) secured the water rights to Yawgoog and Wincheck Ponds with the purchase. In connection with securing the water rights, it was necessary to secure certain rights owned by the Centerville Mills; therefore, in 1947 Rhode Island Boy Scouts bought the Centerville Mills, after a fire, for $5,500 and executed a lease on the Mills whereby the lessee repaired the property; paid taxes; paid rent; and then bought the property minus the water rights. In 1947 the cost of the Centerville Mills including legal fees and survey was $6,062. After renting the property back to Centerville Mills and receiving an income for rent of $2,500, RIBS sold the property in 1953 for $5,500 resulting in a profit of $1,938, plus ownership of the water rights.

1958

A. Livingston Kelley donated 250 acres (Kelgrant) on the Petaquanscut River in North Kingstown to the Rhode Island Boy Scouts in 1958.

1960

The Golden Jubilee Capital Campaign was held and $500,000 was raised.

1961

W. Chesley Worthington served as Council President in 1961. Chet joined the movement in 1915 and remained an active volunteer until his death in 2002. He began his tenure in Scouting as a member of Third Providence Troop and camped at Yawgoog Scout Reservation during its first season in 1916. As a young Scout, Chet earned the rank of Star Scout and missed Eagle Scout because he did not earn his 'bird study' merit badge. He later joined Troop 33 Providence and in 1926 he became a member of the Third Providence Old Timers Association and served as a member for more than three decades. Chet served several years on the Camp Staff at Yawgoog and also was a past chairman of the Camp Committee. He was an active Board Member of the Narragansett Council through 1966 when he began a thirty-six year term on the Advisory Council. He was awarded the Silver Beaver for Distinguished Service to Youth in 1953. Chet was a trustee of the Rhode Island Boy Scouts from 1949 to his death in 2002.

1962 to 1972—Robert F. Parkinson, Scout Executive

Robert F. "Parky" Parkinson earned his Eagle Badge on 4/17/35 as a member of Troop 8 Pawtucket. He served as Assistant Scoutmaster and Scoutmaster for the troop from 1936 to 1941. Bob attended Brown University receiving an AB Degree before enlisting in the Air Force. He was a B-17 Bomber pilot in the 8th Air Force and served as Operations Officer and Squadron Commander. He received the Distinguished Flying Cross with cluster and the Air Medal with 5 clusters. Parky attended the 119th National BSA Training School and his first job was as a District Executive with the Nausau County Council. He then went on to serve as a DE and a Director of Camping Activities with the Otetiana Council. He served as Director of Camp Massawepie Scout Camp in 1951 and 1953. His first job as a Scout Executive was with the Ridgewood Glen Rock Council in New Jersey and then with the Manhattan Council in New York City. Parky came to the Narragansett Council in 1962 and served as Scout Executive until 1972. He was transferred to the Trans Atlantic Council in Germany in late 1972. Parky was married to Ethel Ainsworth and upon retiring, they moved to Alachua, Florida. He passed away on August 9th, 1995.

1962

At Camp Aquapaug, Tucker Shelter, built at a cost of $2,000 donated by Mrs. Howard W. Tucker of South Kingstown, was dedicated on November 3, 1962. Members of the King Philip Camp Advisory Committee built a water system to provide running water at the Buxton Lodge.

At a special meeting on November 1, 1962, the Rhode Island Boy Scouts approved the purchase of the Fisher Land, approximately 100 acres of woodland, adjoining our property on the southeast, with frontage on Wincheck Pond and Long Bridge Road at Yawgoog. RIBS also approved the purchase of Mrs. Clifford Palmer's property on the same road leading to the camp gate, about 1500 feet from the gate, with approximately 325 feet frontage on the road and the same frontage on Wincheck Pond.

Membership reaches 20,203 Cub Scouts, Boy Scouts and Explorers.

1963

Rhode Island Boy Scouts signed the agreement with the Providence Redevelopment Agency for the Scout Center land on May 27, 1963. A contract was executed with Sterling Engineering and Construction Company, Inc. for the construction of the new Scout Center on Broad and Stewart Streets on October 10, 1963. The architect who designed the new Scout Center was D. Thomas Russillo, A.I.A.

In 1963 Yawgoog moved from 4th place to 2nd place in the National rating of councils our size. Improvements to Yawgoog in 1963 included enlarging the Ranger's House by two bedrooms and one bath; Health Lodge floor completely replaced and many trees removed to keep it dryer; two drain fields built, one at Bucklin and one at Three Point; built a new 20-boat sailing dock; built 15 new tent platforms; and, enlarged our fleet by 8 canoes, three rowboats and 3 sailboats.

Champlin Reservation was very heavily used in 1963 with more than 1,000 boys and leaders using it every month of the year. Improvements made to Champlin in 1963 included: security fencing; fire equipment and fire lanes improved; new water pump in the Ranger's House; parking lot resurfaced and some road improved; and, 20 new campsites cut out for expanded camping service.

In 1963 the Rhode Island Boy Scouts approved the sale of Whipple Highlands (38 acres) to the Town of North Providence for $24,000

1964

The new Council Service center on 175 Broad Street, Providence was dedicated—14,000 square feet—with land purchased from the State of Rhode Island and the Providence Redevelopment Agency.

Woonsocket Area Boy Scout Foundation voted to deed the 175-acre Winnesucket Property to the Rhode Island Boy Scouts and the deed was recorded in May, 1964.

1965

On November 1st, 1965, a special meeting of the Rhode Island Boy Scouts was called with the specific purpose of the meeting to act on a proposed agreement regarding the relationship of Rhode Island Boy Scouts and Narragansett Council, Boy Scouts of America, especially in the matter of properties and trust funds. The proposed agreement, the first draft of which had been prepared in 1963, had finally been worked out by a sub-committee of Rhode Island Boy Scouts, consisting of Messrs. Clapp, Dewing and Williams, after conferences with a committee of Narragansett Council, composed of Avery Seaman and Philip M. Shires, with President Phillips D. Booth and Scout Executive Robert F. Parkinson also present. The agreement had been approved by the Executive Committee of Narragansett Council. The motion was put and those in favor were Messrs. Clapp, Dewing, Goff, Haffenreffer, Horton, Lownes, Nicholson, Palmer, Viall and Williams. Mr. Brown was opposed. It was declared that the vote had passed to approve the agreement to consummate it with Narragansett Council Boy Scouts of America.

1966

John A. Horton served as Narragansett Council President from 1966 to 1968. As a young boy, John was a Scout and earned the rank of 2nd Class. He became an active volunteer in Scouting and served the youth of the Narragansett Council until his death in 2002. He was the founder and CEO of Horton, Church & Goff, Inc. from 1954 until he retired in 1980. He was an active community leader with directorships with Citizens Financial Group, Providence Mutual Insurance Company and Rhode Island Industrial Foundation. John received the Silver Beaver Award in 1967 for his Distinguished Service to Youth.

Dr. Raymond F. Hacking who was known as 'the first Boy Scout in Rhode Island' passed away in 1966 and Roger W. Kenyon, Yawgoog workman for nearly 30 years, retired because of illness.

Arthur W. Leidman, member of Narragansett Council staff since 1928, retired on December 1, 1966. An Endowment Fund Program was established by the RIBS in 1966.

1967

Simon R. Sands, Jr. and Virginia Sands Critchell, wife of former Blackstone District Executive Robert E. Critchell, offered to give the Boy Scouts 20 to 30 acres of land adjacent to the eastern end of the airport runway on Block Island if the Scouts paid the back taxes of $364.80. This land was accepted by Narragansett

Council and Rhode Island Boy Scouts, the tax bill was paid and the deed recorded in the name of Rhode Island Boy Scouts. This property would become Sandsland.

1968

At a Special Meeting of the Rhode Island Boy Scouts, it was voted to form "Rhode Island Boy Scouts, A Connecticut Corporation" for the purpose of holding title to the real estate of the corporation in the State of Connecticut and that upon creation of such corporation, all real estate of the corporation located in the State of Connecticut be conveyed to said corporation and further that the officers of the corporation be and each of them hereby is authorized to execute such documents and deeds and to such other acts as are necessary or convenient to carry out the foregoing".

The Rhode Island Boy Scouts office was located at 1426 Industrial Bank Building in Providence, Rhode Island, for 6 ½ years. The bank informed RIBS that it would be needing the space as of December 31, 1968 so space was provided for RIBS to have an office at the Scout Center at 175 Broad Street, Providence, Rhode Island.

Gordon Perrin of Ashaway performed the original installation of the pumping and storage system of the Yawgoog water supply. Weston and Sampson, engineers of Boston, also advised on the original job. Also at Yawgoog, a waste disposal engineering study, along with conferences with the Boy Scout Engineering Service, Weston and Sampson, The Seabees and the State Chief of Water Pollution, suggested that the Council construct an improved grease trap and a leaching field at Three Point. The State approved the project and similar fields were constructed at Medicine Bow and Sandy Beach.

The old Troop 15 Providence campsite located in Foster, Rhode Island, was sold for a sum of $5,500 in 1968.

During 1967 and 1968, the Council was fortunate to enlarge the 175 acre Camp Winnesuket in the Towns of Burrillville, Rhode Island, and Thompson, Connecticut, to a total of 1800 acres . . . thus Buck Hill Scout Reservation was born. The property included three existing lakes and had a potential for two more by reconstructing dams and flooding marshlands which were ponds about 100 years ago. The reservation was unique in that it bordered three state parks with a total of 5000 acres greatly enhancing the hiking and outpost camping potential. The plan at the time of purchase was to construct seven camps by the year 2000. Camp A (Winnesuket) was to be completed by 1970; Camp B (Murray Hill) was to be completed by 1975; Camp C by 1980; Camp D by 1985; Camp E by 1990; Camp F by 1995; and, Camp G by 2000.

1969

H. Cushman "Gus" Anthony retired from Professional Scouting on March 1, 1969 but continued his volunteer work with Narragansett Council until the day he passed away.

Elmer S. Horton resigned as a member of RIBS. He had served since 1948. Here was his tribute: "Your connection with Scouting goes back to the days when you were a Troop Committeeman of Troop 2 Barrington in 1929. You became a power of Scouting in the thirties when you served as Chairman of the Bristol County District and a member of the Board of Directors of Narragansett Council. Then you began to head up the Public Relations activities of the Council and helped to develop that wonderful "How Book of Public Relations", which made Narragansett Council nationally famous and which led to an invitation to speak at the national Council meeting. In 1940 you became Vice President of the Council and in 1948, the President. What a wonderful Council leader you made and how Narragansett Council leapt ahead—especially when you convinced Livingston Kelley to head up the Council Survey and the interest which Mr. Kelley developed resulting in the gift of the Kelgrant Reservation. Also in 1948 you became a member of Rhode Island Boy Scouts and you have served this Trustee corporation so well and faithfully ever since with your advice and counsel and your membership on the Investment Committee. Forty years in all as a leader of the greatest boys' organization in the world. What a record! But, 'Once a Scout, always a Scout', and you will forever be on the rolls of Scouting as a Silver Beaver of 1948 and as one of the finest men in the movement and in the lives of hundreds of its men and boys."

Also in 1969, T. Dawson Brown turned over the reins as President of the Rhode Island Boy Scouts to Paul C. Nicholson. The following testimonial was lettered into a picture of the Brown Gateway at Yawgoog and was framed:

T. Dawson Brown
President—Rhode Island Boy Scouts 1927 to 1969

Some men build fences to keep people out!
Some men build gates to let people in!
Such a man is T. Dawson Brown!

A gateway is named for him at Yawgoog Scout Camps, because he opened the portal to adventure, advancement, self-reliance and character to thousands of boys.

But this gate is also a symbol of his lifetime of opening doors or opportunity and promise to human beings, to organizations, to entire communities.

For fifty-eight years he has been a Scout Leader, and for forty-three years he has been President of Rhode Island Boy Scouts.

And all these years, he has been flinging wide the gates—pushing back narrowness, bigotry, littleness—so that vision, comradeship and greatness might enter men's lives.

So, as he concludes his service as President of Rhode Island Boy Scouts, on this fourth day of December, nineteen hundred and sixty nine, his brother Scouts and co-workers hail him and open the gates of their hearts to flood him with their fondest love and appreciation.

The T. Dawson Brown Gate is located at the entrance of Yawgoog at the end of Camp Yawgoog Road and is dedicated to T. Dawson Brown. Two Thunderbirds rest atop the gate—Indian messengers to the Great Spirit and protector of campers. There are also four animals carved into the gate: Fox, Beaver, Owl and Bear.

Enrollment at Yawgoog in 1969 was 5,441 and Donald S. Fowler was named Director of Outdoor Activities replacing H. Cushman Anthony.

The SeaBees under Captain Ide and the National Guard under General Holland provided labor for the development of the first camp at Buck Hill. The camp was named Winnesuket in honor of the old Woonsocket camp there. The new camp opened in 1970.

1970

J. Harold Williams relinquished his bookkeeping and administrative work with the Rhode Island Boy Scouts because of the increasing difficulty of making the frequent necessary trips from Cape Cod to Providence. Mr. Williams proposed that Donald C. Dewing, who was serving as Treasurer, take over the corporation's office and carry on the administrative work.

Prior to 1970 Yawgoog was known as 'Camp Yawgoog". In 1970 the official name became "Yawgoog Scout Reservation" and everything in the Trading Post (t-shirts, hats, cups) was engraved with "Yawgoog Scout Reservation". While today the official name of Yawgoog is still "Yawgoog Scout Reservation" and most items are engraved and sold that way, the camp is still referred to as 'Camp Yawgoog' by many.

1971

The State of Rhode Island took land in the Snake Den section of Johnston for park purposes and offered Rhode Island Boy Scouts $2,900 for its 'Grey Wolf Mine" property of 23.3 acres in the center of the area.

In 1971, 4,783 boys attended Yawgoog, an increase of 151 boys over 1970. The camp operated in the black and produced $8,000.

1972

Clinton L. Armstrong, Camp Yawgoog Ranger 1934-1959 passed away on May 21, 1972 and Edith L. Besser, bookkeeper for the Rhode Island Boy Scouts, also passed away on August 26, 1972.

In 1972 F. C. Pearce Drummond, Richard Viall and Wilfred B. Utter resigned as Members of RIBS. A Salute to Utter, Drummond and Viall was written on December 7, 1972 when they resigned from RIBS: "Hail to three veterans who this day conclude active service in the Boy Scout Movement, but who will continue their deep interest and support with the title-Member Emeritus. Their leadership for Scouting totals more than 150 years. Rhode Island Boy Scouts, which was formed in 1910 to organize the Scout Program in our State and which has maintained its identity ever since—first as an administrative organization and in later years as a Trustee Group—recognized the loyalty, devotion and accomplishments of these men with joy, pride and honor.

Their names have already been registered in the written History of Rhode Island Scouting, but this day we shall record this memorial in the archives of our corporation so that those who come after may know of our deep appreciation, esteem and affection for them." Following is a brief bio on all three men:

Wilfred B. Utter became famous in Scouting when he, as a Scoutmaster in Westerly, brought the first Troop to Camp Yawgoog when it opened in 1916. Following success as a troop leader, he became District Commissioner for Westerly and then Chairman of the Quequatuck District and a member of Narragansett Council Board of Directors. He was awarded the Silver Beaver for distinguished service to boyhood in 1946. In 1957, Wilfred became a member of Rhode Island Boy Scouts, taking the place of his deceased brother George Benjamin Utter. Wilfred Utter lives the code of the Scout Law and it can be truly said that he is "a friend to all and a brother to every other Scout".

F.C. Pearce Drummond came into Scouting in 1922 at the invitation of Scout Commissioner Donald S. Babcock, with whom he had served in World War I. He became a District Commissioner, visiting and helping Troops in Providence and vicinity. His work was so outstanding that, in 1926, he was elected Commissioner of the Council, holding that post for five years. In 1933, he became President of Narragansett Council, succeeding T. Dawson Brown and holding that office for five years also. He received the Silver Beaver in 1945. His membership in this corporation goes back to 1926. A man of true patriotism, positive convictions, tremendous energy and firm faith, Pearce Drummond has been a great leader of men.

Richmond Viall had distinguished service as an aviator in the First World War. Returning to civilian life he joined his friends Everett Hartwell, Maurice Congdon, T. Dawson Brown, Charles Marshall and others in the nineteen twenties in service on the Council Board. He became a member of RIBS in 1935. When Everett Hartwell, of beloved memory, gathered all our funds together in 1950 to set up our Endowment Fund and Agency Account, Richie became one of the members of the new Investment Committee. After Everett Hartwell's death in 1954, Richie succeeded him as Chairman and held that position until he resigned this fall. Through his labors, our income from investments has greatly increased. His efforts for Scouting have always matched his enthusiasm and joy of living. May the Lord be praised for the careers of Utter, Drummond and Viall.

The RIBS Trustees voted Aaron H. Roitman, Past President of Narragansett Council and General Chairman of the Golden Jubilee Campaign, to replace Wilfred Utter; Charles E. Clapp, 2nd, Attorney at Law was voted to replace Richmond Viall; and, Arthur E. Nelson, Assistant Tax Manager, ITT-Grinnell Corporation, replaced F. C. Pearce Drummond.

1973 to 1990—Vincent N. Borrelli, Scout Executive

Vince Borrelli was born in Minersville, Pennsylvania, and attended Minersville High School. Vince began his Scouting career in Pottsville, PA, served as a Patrol Leader and attained the rank of Star Scout. He graduated from Lock Haven State University with a B.S. Degree in Education with majors in Physical Education and Biology and a minor in General Science. Vince served in the Army, graduating Officer Training School at Fort Reilly, KS and became a Military Training Officer. Vince served in Korea and remained in the Army Reserves until 1963 attaining the rank of Captain.

Vince entered Professional Scouting in 1953 serving as District Executive and Field Director in various councils and became Scout Executive of Bucktail Council in Dubois, PA in 1965. He served as Deputy Scout Executive of Baltimore Area Council until he was promoted to Scout Executive of Narragansett Council on April 1st, 1973. His 17 year tenure as Scout Executive in the Narragansett Council is chuck full of great leaders, membership growth, financial stability and great new initiatives. Vince retired from the Narragansett Council in 1990 and he and his wife 'Ginny' live in Johnston, Rhode Island. Vince retired and became a farmer growing everything from Christmas Trees to strawberries. Vince and Ginny own and operate Long Pond Farm.

Vincent N. Borrelli and his wife Virginia "Ginny" Borrelli

THE JACQUES E. DUBOIS YEARS
Council President—1973 to 1975

On January first, 1973, Jacques E. Dubois became President of Narragansett Council, and as President, his first job was to secure a new Scout Executive. Vincent N. Borrelli, Director of Field Service in Baltimore, MD, was interviewed and hired. His tenure began on April first, 1973.

Now that the new Scout Executive was hired, the next step was to establish a five year plan. Charles E. Clapp, II, immediate Past President chaired the Planning Committee and the following goals were approved:

1. Restructure the Council to reduce districts from twelve to eight
2. Eliminate two satellite offices—Newport and Pawtucket
3. Reduce the Professional Staff from twenty to seventeen

The changes in redistricting and staffing were accomplished soon after the new Scout Executive was in place. The office closings were accomplished by district votes under the leadership of Ed Coderre and John Johnson a little later on in 1973.

In the fall of 1973 two major events took place. John "Jake" Harvey became the Director of Field Service and a Trading Post was established as part of the Service Center. Bill Dyer, former District Executive of the Newport District, became the first Trading Post Manager. Jake Harvey's service to Narragansett Council in membership and sustaining membership were a major factor in the Council's success. During 1973 and 1974, the Council continued to implement the changes included in the five year plan.

Jack Dubois' influence went far beyond his membership on the Board of the Rhode Island Boy Scouts or as President of the Narragansett Council. He was thoughtful, enthusiastic and constant in his discussions and action.

Jack was a veteran of 50 lively years in Scouting. He served on the Troop Committee of his six sons' troop and was its chairman. He chaired his District Committee. As President of Scouting's New England Area 1, he led 29 councils in the largest Area in the United States. He was Subcamp Program Director in three successive quadrennial National Scout Jamborees (1977, 1981 and 1985); and in 1989 was Subcamp Program Director. He had been a member of the National Camp Inspectors Team and a Course Director at Philmont. His many Scouting honors include the Wood Badge, the St. George Medal, the Scouter's Key, the Silver Beaver and the Silver Antelope. He, along with such greats as General Colin L. Powell and James A. Lovell, Jr., received the Silver Buffalo Award at the 1992 National Council Meeting in Cincinnati, Ohio. Jack was equally proud of his Eagle Scout sons and his wife, Lucille, who shared his commitment to Scouting. The Council flourished during the Dubois Years with membership in the Council at the end of 1975 totaling 21,877, a gain of 222 members over the previous years.

Jack Dubois died on November 3rd, 1998 and then Council President Andrew Erickson summed up Jack's life the best: "His enthusiasm and dedication to Scouting and his belief in the endowment of our local Council were unsurpassed. His leadership and generosity brought about the birth and strength of our Fleur-de-lis opportunity. So, with a heavy heart we say goodbye to a man who took his Scouting oath seriously, in every aspect of his life. He and his work will long be remembered."

1973

The Scout Center Trading Post was added to the Scout Office at 175 Broad Street, Providence, Rhode Island.

1974

The Tree Farm at Yawgoog began with a grant from The Champlin Foundations in 1974. The Training Lodge at Champlin was completed.

1975

Morris Gaebe donated $12,000 for a Log Cabin at Yawgoog in honor of his four Eagle Scout sons to be used for winter camping and for the Protestant Chaplain quarters in the summer.

Greg, Geoff (Mom Audrey) John and Dana Gaebe
The Four Eagles Cabin at Yawgoog was erected in 1977 in honor of the four
Gaebe Eagle Scouts from Troop 2 Barrington—a gift from their parents.
The cabin is also referred to as the 'Parsonage'—the
summer residence of the Protestant Chaplain.

Dr. Morris J.W. Gaebe and grandsons Glen and JT
(sons of Dana Gaebe)

THE GEORGE B. ROORBACH YEARS
Council President—1976 to 1978

The Roorbach years were filled with many challenges. During Roorbach's term, J. Harold Williams and T. Dawson Brown passed away; Mike DeCiantis resigned as Council Commissioner; Buck Hill became a Family Campground; all of the Council's properties were designated as Tree Farms; and the Richmond "Wood Lot" and Kelgrant were sold.

When Mike DeCiantis resigned as Council Commissioner, Jules A. Cohen agreed to serve as his replacement. Jules was no stranger to Scouting as he had served as a Cubmaster, District Chairman and the Assistant Council Commissioner.

After a usage study was done on all the properties owned by the Council and the Rhode Island Boy Scouts, Kelgrant and the Richmond "Wood Lot" were deemed to be of no value to the Scouting Program, thus excess properties. With the expert help of our legal counsel, Charles J. McGovern, both properties were sold.

After two years of trying to save the Buck Hill Campground, it became apparent that Buck Hill could no longer sustain its summer operations. In 1976 a revised plan of operation was conceived to convert the camp into a Scout Family Campground. This plan gave future administrations of the Narragansett Council the option to explore other uses for the camp.

Through a grant from the Rhode Island Boy Scouts, Tree Farms were developed at Yawgoog and Buck Hill. The grant also provided for the hiring of a ranger at Yawgoog to work the Tree Farm, a new tractor and dump truck at Yawgoog and a tractor at Buck Hill.

Changes in the Rhode Island Boy Scouts also took place during Roorbach's term as Council President. Paul C. Nicholson, Jr. became the President and Vincent N. Borrelli became its second Secretary. Changes in the By-Laws were made to include the President, Finance Vice President and Treasurer of the Narragansett Council as voting members of RIBS. Also, the current serving Scout Executive of the Narragansett Council would also serve as the Secretary of the Rhode Island Boy Scouts and RIBS audit reports, as required by each Council, would be sent to the National Council Boy Scouts of America.

Camping at Yawgoog flourished under the leadership of Al Mink as Reservation Director. Troops in Connecticut and Long Island discovered Yawgoog. Word spread and more and more units from other Councils began to use Yawgoog as their summer camp. The great support from George Roorbach and volunteers like Bob Pease, Mel Hoffman, Stan Turco, Jules Cohen and the entire Executive Board made it all possible.

1976

J. Harold Williams "Chief" passed away on March 21st, 1976.

At the RIBS Annual Meeting in 1976, it was voted to liquidate the Yawgo Line and Twine Company as a separate corporate entity as, in fact, the separate corporation has resulted in a duplication of reports and returns and the payment of an unnecessary Rhode Island Franchise Tax.

1977

The Richmond Property was sold to Messrs. Cohen and Larogue for the purchase price of $132,000.

Robert Hathaway Goff passed away on July 4, 1977. He was Chairman of the Investment Committee of the Rhode Island Boy Scouts.

In 1977 under the guidance of William A. "Wild Bill" Sandford, 'retired' volunteers formed a group called the **OVER THE HILL GANG**. The basic premise of the group was to be at the beck and call of the Narragansett Council Office to offer assistance, stuff envelopes and prepare mailings. Current members include: Kenneth Baker, Robert Barnes, Walter Berger, William Bivona, Vincent N. Borrelli, Jules A. Cohen, Don Crout, Henry K. Delovio, Joseph V. DeStefano, Andrew M. Erickson, Paul Feeney, Robert "Bob" Fricker, Pauline Fricker, Bernie George, Donald Hanson, Arthur W. Keegan, Robert Liptrot, Alfred "Gus" Pagel, Clifford W. Sjoberg, Irwin Talbot and Thomas Wallace. Staff Liaison: Diane Cloutier

IN MEMORY: Deceased members of the "Over the Hill Gang".
William A. Sandford, Fearless Leader and Founder of the 'Over the Hill Gang'.

Sander F. Wilson	W. Allison Berger	Lester Salisbury
J. Edward Howarth	William McComb	Joseph E. Gerstenlauer
James Pennell	Elwyn Mitchell	Stanley R. Bamforth
Roy A. Morrish	H. Cushman "Gus" Anthony	Donald Maker
Eli Jose	Chester Bruno	Edward McManus
John Maloney	Eugene Verrier	Malcolm Daniels
Warren Grogan	Paul Valletta	Stanley F. Turco
	Gilbert Giles	Henry P. Shepard

1978

Rhode Island Boy Scouts sold the Anderson Property (96 acres in Connecticut) at Buck Hill netting $89,457.70 and the Kelgrant Property for $150,000. The Anderson Property was sold to Mr.& Mrs. Howard Swearer and Kelgrant was sold to Henry E. Kates. It was determined by the Council that the Anderson, Kelgrant and Richmond properties were not needed for the camping program of Narragansett Council.

Albert Edgar Lownes died in November of 1978. Al Lownes, Vice President and member of the Rhode Island Boy Scouts, transferred title to the 250 acres of Aquapaug to the Scouts in the hopes that Aquapaug would be used as a camping outpost and as a wildlife and botanical sanctuary.

THE STANLEY F. TURCO YEARS
Council President—1979 to 1981

In 1979 Stan Turco was elected Council President and his Vice Presidents were Herb Cummings, Tullio DeRobbio, J. Russell Gray and Bob Pease. Jules Cohen served as Council Commissioner. In the mid seventies the Council began conducting Council Coordinated meetings. These meetings gave Council operating committee members, Commissioner Staff members and District Chairmen the opportunity to come together at the Council Office. As these meetings evolved, attendance began to grow and the morale of the volunteers and staff alike began to improve dramatically. The new Exploring Division, with Ray Stockard as Chairman, and the new Special Scouting Committee, led by Vahram Tashjian, gave the Council a full table of organization and a boost to membership.

In 1980, Stan Turco and Jack Dubois organized the Fleur-de-lis Club in an effort to begin to solicit endowment gifts for the Council. From its humble beginnings, the Endowment Funds in the Council have grown to become one of the principal parts of the financing of our Council. The basis of this endowment growth came from a gift from Bob and Dotty Pease.

Camping at Yawgoog was growing. Camp attendance now included 40 percent of out of council troops. Yawgoog was operating at optimum level and paying its own way. This was also true of the Buck Hill Family Campground and the Cub Day Camps.

In 1989, the second long range plan was being formulated. Facilities at Yawgoog began to expand. The Kelly Nature Center, Galkin Cabin for Handicapped Scouts, the Four Eagles Cabin (Gaebe), the Fuller Cabin, the Jewish Temple, the Latner Cabin, the new Ranger's Cabin and the new Director's Cabin were built. A new handicapped campsite was constructed and several new camp sites were established to expand our camping capability. The ropes course was constructed and all facilities for administration and program were brought into first class shape. In addition to the winter facilities at Yawgoog, two new cabins and a swimming pool were added at Camp Champlin and the Troop Cabin at Buck Hill was refurbished.

In an effort to continue the impact of the Commissioner Staff, Jules Cohen began to conduct "Commissioner Conferences" at Yawgoog. The impact of these events in the Council was a great boost in morale and in district operation. The 'Conferences' were later changed to "Commissioner Colleges" and honorary degrees were awarded. The first degree went to William J. "Bill" Gilbane. This event was good adult training which let to good Scouting for young people.

One of the highlights of the Turco years was the Scout Show held at Lincoln Downs in Lincoln. The show involved Cub Scouts and Explorers under the viewing stands and outside in the track enclosure. The entire infield was covered with Scout units in Scouting Projects. This event was such a success that it was planned every two years since that first show. Narragansett Council began a membership growth that continued into the late 80's. Greater New York Council and Narragansett Council were the only councils in the Northeast Region enjoying membership growth. The foundations built by Dubois, Roorbach and Turco cast a long shadow in the life of Narragansett Council. Stan remained a strong influence on Scouting in the trenches and at the Council level until his death on May 11th, 2010.

Tullio A. DeRobbio

Enlisted to join the Narragansett Council Executive Board in 1979 by Stan Turco, Tullio A. DeRobbio was an astute businessman with a great affection for good food. He was the President and Owner of M. DeRobbio & Sons, Inc., which was a specialty food wholesale business founded in 1912 by his grandfather, father and uncle. Tully was a Scout as a boy in Providence and earned his 1st Class Badge with Troop 49. Once on the Executive Board and with his keen sense of finance, Tullio became a Finance vice President and served many years in that capacity. The Narragansett Council recognized his great works on behalf of Scouting and in 1983 awarded Tully the Silver Beaver for Distinguished Service to Youth. Tullio was a Navy veteran of World War II, the Korean War and the Israel-Arab War of 1948 and was a member of the Navy Reserve from 1953 to 1967. Although Tully was a graduate of Brown University, he served as a president and treasurer of the Rhode Island College Foundation and received the Rhode Island College Alumni Association Service Award. He was Vice President of *Keep Providence Beautiful* and both founder and sponsor of its annual Pasta Challenge. He also served as a director of the Cranston Rotary Club. Tullio became a member of the Rhode Island Boy Scouts in 1996 and served as the Assistant Treasurer and a member of the Investment Committee until his death in November of 2002.

Charles J. McGovern was recruited as a member of the Rhode Island Boy Scouts in 1980 during Stan Turco's term as Council President. As a young man Charlie was a Scout, camped at Yawgoog and earned the rank of Eagle Scout. As an adult he became an active volunteer in Scouting as the Advancement Chairman in the West Shore District and then as a member of the Executive Committee and Board. He was awarded the Silver Beaver in 1981. From his start as an Executive Board member, Charlie became known as the Council's Legal Counsel serving in that position for well over thirty years—all of them pro bono. Charlie was a dedicated Scouter right up until his death in August of 2007.

1979

In 1979 Yawgoog was considered a Regional Boy Scout Camping Center with approximately one-third of the campers coming from out of council locations. Mr. Robert H. Pease chaired the Kelley Memorial Committee to develop a plan for a Kelley Memorial Nature-Ecology Center at Yawgoog. The Camp Director's Cabin was destroyed by fire on May 24, 1979.

The Metcalf-Sharpe Trust was terminated on July 10, 1979 and the assets distributed to various beneficiaries, among them was the Rhode Island Boy Scouts. RIBS received $169,721 in cash and common stock in the amount of $147,647.

The Buck Hill Family Campground became fully operational in 1979.

1980

The Richmond Woodlot was sold by the Rhode Island Boy Scouts for $132,000.

F. C. Pearce Drummond, District Commissioner, Council Commissioner, Narragansett Council President for five years during the years 1933-1937 passed away in May of 1980. Scouting icon T. Dawson Brown passed away on December 16, 1980. Roger T. Clapp, long time Board Member, Past President of the Council and Silver Beaver Recipient passed away on January 8th, 1980.

Repairs to the Bucklin Memorial Building included repairing the stairways, posts and rails, floors refinished and repairs made to the toilet and shower rooms for a total of $20,000.

1981

The Lattner Cabin was constructed at Yawgoog. Gus Anthony organized the first 'Old Timers Reunion' (now the Yawgoog Alumni Association Reunion) at Yawgoog on August 22, 1981, with 400 people in attendance.

Thomas J. Gilbane passed away on November 7th, 1981. Tom was the first Chairman of the National Eagle Scout Association and was one of the two volunteers in the Narragansett Council to receive the Silver Buffalo Award from National. The other recipient was Jacques E. Dubois. Tom received the Silver Buffalo Award in 1980 and Jack received the award in 1992.

THE HERBERT W. CUMMINGS YEARS
Council President—1982 to 1984

In 1982, Herb Cummings became Council President. Tiger Cubs came into being and the Narragansett Council led the Northeast Region in their recruitment. The Commissioner Colleges were a huge success and two hundred and twelve commissioners were in attendance at the College during Herb's first year as President. In 1982, 4,839 Explorers were registered in the Council, all a part of many specialty posts that were organized, many of which are still serving the Council today. Art Gebhardt served as Chairman of the Exploring Division during Herb's tenure and did great work with his committee and the staff.

In 1984, the Council lost its devoted Council Camping Chairman, Dr. Mel Hoffman. Mel's sailboat capsized in a lake in Texas while he was vacationing. Mel was devoted to camping and especially Yawgoog and spent much of his time recruiting doctors for the Yawgoog Staff.

Membership in the Council continued to grow and 1983 marked the fifth year of continued growth. The volunteer and professional teams serving the Council at this time were stable and effective. There were many great packs, troops and posts in operation. 1983 also marked the promotion of John Harvey to Scout Executive of Utica, New York. His work in Commissioner Service, Sustaining Membership and staff leadership was a credit to our profession. Don Reinhardt was promoted to Director of Field Service to replace Jake.

MEMBERS OF THE RHODE ISLAND BOY SCOUTS DURING THE EARLY 80'S

Paul C. Nicholson, Jr. President
Charles E. Clapp II, Vice President
Donald C. Dewing, Treasurer
Jacques E. Dubois
R. F. Haffenreffer, III
Louis R. Hampton
John A. Horton
Arthur R. Langlais
Charles J. McGovern
Arthur E. Nelson
Robert H. Pease
Aaron H. Roitman
George B. Roorbach
W. Chesley Worthington

Ex-Officio Members:
Vincent N. Borrelli, Scout Executive and Secretary
Herbert W. Cummings, Council President
Tullio A. DeRobbio, Vice President Finance, NC

1982

The Kelley Nature Center at Yawgoog was constructed in 1982 after the sale of Kelgrant in Narragansett.

The Order of the Arrow dedicated the opening of its Freedom Trail in Newport on April 17th.

The dedication of the newly constructed Herman S. Galkin Memorial Cabin at Yawgoog was held on August 15th, 1982.

The Special Scouting Division was developed in June of 1982.

1983

Former Council President, Phillips D. Booth, passed away in January of 1983.

The Alumni Association completed Project I over the summer including the landscaping of the Donald North Court with 125 Rhododendrons and Arborvitae and the re-shingling of the T. Dawson Brown Gateway and the re-shingling of the Brown Fountain, at a total cost of $2,300.

Two other events occurred in 1983. H. Cushman "Gus" Anthony organized the Yawgoog Alumni Association, which became a valuable part of Scouting in the

Narragansett Council. The Association collects membership dues and conducts fund—raising initiatives to improve camp facilities at Yawgoog. The second event was the hiring of Judy Ferrante as secretary to the Scout Executive. She soon became secretary to the Yawgoog Alumni Association as well and continues in that capacity to this day. As of this writing, she has been Administrative Assistant to five Scout Executives in her 29 years of service to the Narragansett Council.

Capital improvements made throughout the Council properties in 1983 included the completion of the Kelley Nature Center; the acquisition of thirty new boats and canoes; the repair and replacement of the heating system at the Bucklin Building; the repair of the stone stairs on the Donald North Court side of the Bucklin Building; the complete renovation of the Sandy Beach Dining Hall and kitchen; and, a new truck and tractor at Buck Hill.

Jacques E. Dubois, Chairman of the Planned Giving Committee, introduced and organized the 'Fleur-de-lis Club' for endowment development, with a gift of cash, insurance, property, trusts or other charitable instrument to the Endowment Fund of the Narragansett Council required for membership into the club.

1984

The Executive Committee authorized the hiring of the first two para-professionals in the Narragansett Council. One was to serve the Hmung community and the other to serve the Hispanic community. Varsity Scouting was also introduced to local councils in 1984.

This year's Yawgoog Alumni Association Project was the refurbishing of the J. Harold Williams Amphitheatre; new totem poles and the planting of approximately 130 shrubs and trees in the Amphitheatre to create a natural screen from the camp road.

Dr. Melvin Hoffman, who served as Camp Yawgoog's Chief Medical Officer for twenty-four years, passed away while on vacation in May of 1984. A scholarship fund for a deserving staff member at Yawgoog was developed from the money donated in memory of Dr. Hoffman.

J. Russell Gray, who served Scouting in many capacities including Vice President of Relationships and Chairman of the High Court of Honor passed away on June 22, 1984.

In October of 1984 the Executive Board approved the Career Awareness Explorer Program to be operational in the Narragansett Council. The Council established the National Eagle Scout Association in 1984 and held its first reception on November 2nd, 1984.

Mr. Jack Feinerman from Boca Raton, Florida, donated 56 acres of land adjoining the Tree Farm on the south boundary of Yawgoog. The Rhode Island Boy Scouts approved the sale of 28 acres of land on the western side of Scituate Avenue of Champlin Scout Reservation to Frank Paolino Construction Company for the sum of $354,830.

THE JULES A. COHEN YEARS
Council President—1985 to 1988

Jules first served Scouting as a Cubmaster, then as Chairman of the West Shore District (Warwick and East Greenwich). He and his father were District Chairmen at the same time in the mid-seventies, Jules for West Shore District and his dad for Pokanoket District. Then, in 1985, Jules became Council President and Arthur Keegan was elected to serve as Council Commissioner. After the death of Donald C. Dewing, Arthur Langlais became Council Treasurer. With his help, the Council employed Victor Castelli, CPA to work with Kathy Santilli and Anne Healey, the Council bookkeepers. Victor Castelli reviewed the Council's statement each month and with this close supervision, the Executive Board was given an accurate finance statement every month.

In the eighties, District Executive Steve Whitney recruited Joseph V. DeStefano to serve as Providence District Chairman. Joe was Vice Principal of Central High School and knew the city well. With Dan Vargas as District Commissioner, Providence District did a good job of managing its Cub and Scout Programs. Membership continued to grow and in 1985, Narragansett Council became the largest council in membership in the New England area. The Council was operating the youth programs effectively and efficiently and balancing the budget.

In 1988, Narragansett Council held its first "Scouting for Food" Drive. Joe DeStefano was the first Chairman. The weekend of the bag delivery went well but the pick-up weekend was another story. It poured rain on Saturday and then again on Sunday. Delivery of the food boxes from the districts to the Food Bank in West Warwick was done by the National Guard. The distribution room was almost bare of food stuffs before the returns began to come in. On Sunday at five o'clock the Food Bank was completely filled. The "Annual Report" for that year stated that "Saturday, November 19th was the day 245 packs, troops and posts made Scouting for Food Good Turn a real success. The Narragansett Council collected 324,000 pounds of food for the Rhode Island Food Bank". The Council's support of the Food Bank continues to this day and Joe DeStefano still serves as the Chairman of the event.

In 1988, the Council achieved an all-time high in Sustaining Membership donations under the leadership of Andrew M. Erickson.

1985

Project III for the Yawgoog Alumni Association was the addition of a Museum at Yawgoog.

Narragansett Council established a National Eagle Scout Association within the Council.

Gus Anthony was elected to the Rhode Island Heritage Hall of Fame.

Hurricane Gloria passed through Rhode Island in September and all camps were closed to camping. Most of the damage consisted of downed trees and debris. Yawgoog was hit the hardest with extensive tree damage and extensive damage to the electric system. Latrines, tent platforms, power lines and poles were all damaged.

The Rhode Island Boy Scouts purchased the Gordon Property (Grassy Pond) consisting of 250 acres of land abutting Yawgoog on the Northeast side of camp. With the addition of the Gordon Land and the gift of 57 acres from Jack Feinerman, Yawgoog Scout Reservation totaled more than 1,700 acres in 1985.

1986

At the January 18th, 1986, Annual Meeting, Donald C. Dewing, who served as Treasurer of the Narragansett Council for 31 years, turned the reins over to Arthur R. Langlais. During Mr. Dewing's tenure as Treasurer, the Council grew from 15,268 to 20,697 members and the budget grew from $82,000 (1955) to $879,300 (1986).

In 1986 Narragansett Council was approved to become a full Scout Distributor by the National Council and Reggie Gaudet joined the Narragansett Council Staff as the first Trading Post Manager of the Scout Shop.

The Cub Scout Task Force recommended and the Executive Board approved training before commissioning for new Cub Leaders, requiring all new leaders being recruited complete Fast Start or Basic Training before assuming the position of Cubmaster, Den Leader, Webelos Leader or Committee Chairman.

1987

Also in 1987, the Council became fully computerized in Registration and Sustaining Membership and other general reports generated by the Council.

On the evening of September 8th, 1987, the Narragansett Cabin at Yawgoog burned down to the ground. The Fire Marshall determined the fire was caused by an electrical short in the building. A new cabin was later built on Pendleton Hill Road as a Ranger House to secure the north end of the camp.

Narragansett Council's 'Special Scouting Division' chaired by Keith Marsello was highlighted in the 75th Anniversary issue of 'Scouting Magazine".

Capital improvements at Yawgoog included a new leach field at the Sandy Beach dining Hall and the complete renovation of the Three Point Dining Hall completed with a grant from The Champlin Foundation. The Training Lodge at Champlin was also refurbished with a grant from The Champlin Foundation.

1988

Bob Barnes takes over the leadership as Council Commissioner from outgoing Council Commissioner, Arthur W. Keegan. Jules A. Cohen is President of Narragansett Council and Arthur R. Langlais holds the title of Treasurer. The Council moved finance management into the computer in its final stage of computerizing the entire Council operation.

The Council conducted two Good Turns in 1988. The first was a tree planting where over 100 Boy Scout Troops planted between 20 and 30 thousand trees at various locations in the State of Rhode Island. The second Good Turn was 'Scouting for Food' where Scouts collected food door to door and the National Guard delivered the food to the Rhode Island Food Bank. Chaired by Joe DeStefano, the first drive netted over 324,000 pounds of food. In 2010 over 280,000 pounds of food was collected as a result of the 23rd Scouting for Food Good Turn.

2006—The hustle and bustle of collecting and boxing the food for the
Rhode Island National Guard to pick up and deliver to the Rhode Island
Food Bank.

The Yawgoog Alumni Association completed Phase 1 of the reconstructed Crafts Center. It was dedicated on July 30th, 1988, in the name of H. Cushman Anthony. Phase II of the H. Cushman Anthony Stockade was under construction at the end of 1988 and was completed for the Diamond Jubilee Celebration in 1990. All four pavilions were donated.

A Buck Hill Study Committee was formed in March of 1987 to study the feasibility of the proposal from Nature Conservancy to purchase the development rights of the Council's Buck Hill Property. The Buck Hill Study Committee and the Executive Committee members voted not to accept the offer of the Nature Conservancy to purchase the development rights for Buck Hill for $750,000. Both Committees also voted not to sell the development rights on sections of parcels of the Buck Hill Property. The Committees developed the following Policy Statement: "It has been the general and ongoing policy of the Boy Scouts of America, and in particular Narragansett Council, to protect the natural environment. We accomplish this by being conscientious stewards of the lands under our control and by the training programs delivered to our members both youth and adult. It is also policy of the Narragansett Council to plan and provide for the future needs of the Scouting Program. This policy would preclude the outright sale or sale of the development rights to portions of the properties. We realize the unique value of the parcels you have made reference to at Buck Hill. The Executive Board of the Narragansett Council then reaffirms the policy of environmental conservation in the future with particular emphasis on the protection of our unique wetlands at Buck Hill."

Several new policies were enacted by action of the National Executive Board in 1988. One of the new policies instructed that trips and outings may not be led by only one adult. At least two adult leaders, one of whom must be 21 years or older, are required for all trips or outings. It is the responsibility of the chartered organization of any pack, troop, team or post/ship to inform the committees and leadership of the units which they sponsor that sufficient adult leadership be provided on all trips and outings. This new policy also incorporates the 'safety rule of four' that requires no less than four individuals (always with a minimum of two adults) on any trip into the 'backcountry' while camping out. If an accident occurs, one person should stay with the injured and two people should go for help. Additional adult leadership requirements must reflect an awareness of such factors as size and skill level of the group, anticipated environmental conditions and overall degree of challenge. A second policy that went into effect provided for female leadership in the Boy Scouts of America.

Longtime Treasurer of Rhode Island Boy Scouts and Narragansett Council, Donald C. Dewing, passed away in December of 1988. Don also served as the Scoutmaster of Troop 82 Providence for 65 years.

THE JONATHAN K. FARNUM YEARS
Council President—1989 to 1991

Jon Farnum became Council President in 1989. Just prior to his election in 1988, all but two of the Council's Professional Staff members changed positions. Albert E. Mink, who had served as Reservation Director at Yawgoog for many years, left the staff in May of 1987 and William J. Burns III was selected to replace him. Bill served as Reservation Director in 1987 and 1988. Paul Boisvert, Scoutmaster of Troop 1 in Warwick, joined the Narragansett Council Staff and became Reservation Director in 1989. All operating committees were functioning and the Council was doing well financially. In November of 1989, Donald Reinhardt, the Council's Director of Field Service was promoted to Scout Executive of the Moby Dick Council.

Other key people who gave service to Narragansett Council during Jon's tenure as President were Bob Fricker who served as District Commissioner, District Chairman of Pokanoket District and Council Activities Chairman; Joe Bottone, District Chairman of Quequatuck District; Al Bucci, Council Membership Chairman; Walter Coupe, Investment Committee Chairman and member of the Rhode Island Boy Scouts; Bill Follett, Campmaster at Aquapaug; Larry Jette, District Commissioner Blackstone Valley District, Chairman of the Council Campmaster Corps (Larry was also known for his great chicken barbeques at Yawgoog); Cdr. Carlton Johnson, Council Eagle Scout Association Chairman; Bill LaLonde, Council Explorer Division Chairman; Richard Lapan, Council Advancement Chairman; Lisolotte Poissant, Council and District Cub Leader; and Charles J. McGovern, Legal Counsel for the Council.

Some key members of the Professional Staff were Mary Ellen Fuller, Director of the Exploring Division, Gale Follett, Director of Special Scouting and Don Crout, Council Program Director.

1989

In 1989, Jonathan K. Farnum was elected Council President and Bob Barnes was Council Commissioner.

Newport Cub Scout David Birdy was featured in Boys' Life Magazine as a recipient of the Heroism Award from the National Council because of his courage and quick thinking when his father severely lacerated his arms after falling through a glass door.

The dam at Buck Hill was repaired by cementing the outflow pipe of the dam to plug up existing leaks. Stones were replaced and the dam was topped with loam and grass seed.

On October 12, 1989, the Executive Board approved the following Affirmative Action Policy: "Narragansett Council offers equal opportunity in employment, training, development, advancement and pay on the basis of qualifications and ability without regard to race, color, national origin, sex, age, religion or handicap. In addition, under Title VII of the 1964 Civil Rights Act, the law seeks to correct past injustices through Affirmative Action. The Boy Scouts of America has defined an Affirmative Action Program which this council has agreed to implement and conduct on an ongoing basis."

The Council had 57 members in the Fleur-de-lis Club in 1989. The H. Cushman Anthony Crafts Center was completed and the four pavilions donated by Dr. Norman Cowen, The Shine Brothers, The Gilbanes & Choquettes, and the Rhode Island Elks Association, were dedicated at the Yawgoog Alumni Association's Annual Meeting at Yawgoog on July 29th.

A new adult application was developed by the National Council which mandated that sponsoring organizations must approve the adult leaders for the Scout units they sponsor. This new adult application caused some dissension among sponsoring organizations and Scouting. On September 1st, 1989, National promoted changes to the Boy Scout Program. A new troop organization plan was introduced calling for the organization of the Tenderfoot Patrol under the leadership of the Assistant Scoutmaster.

The Boy Scouts are finding that boys coming over from the Cub Scout Program into a regular Boy Scout Troop are not easily assimilated into the troop, therefore the Tenderfoot Patrol will take this group of new boys and work with them through the Tenderfoot Second and First Class requirements, or until they are assimilated into the troop structure.

Two new scholarships were implemented for Scouts in the Narragansett Council. A Gilbane Scholarship was established at Johnson & Wales College for students with a Scouting background and a scholarship was established at the Community College of Rhode Island also for students with a Scouting background.

The Zenas Family donated six acres of land completely surrounded by Yawgoog property on the southwest corner of the property near Wincheck Pond.

1990 to 1993—Roy L. Williams, Scout Executive

Roy L. Williams
May 1990 to August 1993

In May of 1990 Roy L. Williams became the fourth Scout Executive of the Narragansett Council. Roy started his career with the BSA in 1972 as a district executive with the Longhorn Council in Fort Worth, Texas. He served as Scout Executive of the Jayhawk Area Council in Topeka, Kansas and as the Director of the Boy Scout Division at the National Council. When Roy completed his tenure here at the Narragansett Council, he became Regional Director for the Western Region located in Tempe, Arizona. From there Roy was named to head the Boy Scouts of America as Chief Scout Executive on June 1, 2000. Roy served as Chief Scout Executive until his retirement on September 1st, 2007. Williams is a graduate of the University of Texas at Arlington, where he received a bachelor's degree in business administration. He and his wife, Barbara, have two children Christi and Andrew.

1990

The Don Cady Campsite, which is handicapped accessible, was ready for the opening of summer camp at Yawgoog in 1990.

1991

The new Learning for Life Program was approved by the Executive Board in October of 1991.

The Yawgoog Alumni Association developed a 9 ½ minute Camp Yawgoog Promotional Video and provided copies for each unit in the council. The YAA's 1991 project was the Refurbishment of the J. Harold Williams Amphitheatre.

1992

Paul J. Choquette, Jr. became Council President and Charles A. Bennett became Council Commissioner. The Urban Initiative Program was developed targeting Providence, Pawtucket, Central Falls, Woonsocket and Newport.

The Department of Health informed the Council that it could no longer use the water from the pond for both swimming and drinking. The course of action to address the matter was to drill for water. Having no luck finding suitable well water, it was decided to use the lake water and build a water treatment plant. Ranger Paul Forbes became the full time certified water treatment operator.

1993 to 1999—Lyle K. Antonides, Scout Executive

Lyle K. Antonides, Scout Executive
September 1993 to December 1999

Lyle K. Antonides became the fifth Scout Executive of the Narragansett Council on September 16th, 1993. Lyle came to Narragansett Council from New York City where he had been the Director of Field Service. Among his many achievements in New York, Lyle expanded membership outreach by 30,000 youth or 38% between 1985 and 1992. He designed and implemented the Urban Scouting emphasis in 1988 for the 'at risk' youth in New York City. He increased fund raising from $460,000 in 1985 to $1,440,000 in 1992; and he led a task force resulting in the decision to build "Cub World" scheduled to open in July 1994. Lyle was in the Scouting Program as a youth as a Cub Scout, Boy Scout and an Eagle Scout. He began his professional career as a District Executive in the Atlantic Area Council and has served as an Exploring Executive, National Director of the National Eagle Scout Association, Communication Director, Director of Exploring, Assistant Director of Field Service and Director of Field Service.

1993

In October of 1993 camping at Block Island was suspended for the remainder of the year because of the Equine Encephalitis problem with mosquitoes.

Extensive work was done on the Buck Hill Dam to correct leaks. Total cost of the repair work was slightly higher than $97,000.

1994

Anthony Gibbs became the Director of Field Service at the Narragansett Council on September 1st, 1994. The Council began its collaboration with the Greater Providence YMCA for use of Camp Buxton for summer camp.

Projects relating to the Capital Campaign were completed in 1994 such as the new roof on the Medicine Bow Dining Hall and replacement of the Medicine Bow Waterfront building.

The first Whitney Young Award Luncheon was held in 1994 and the first honorees were Arthur Robbins and B. Jae Clanton.

1995

Robinson, Green & Beretta was chosen to design Cub World at Buck Hill.

Paul Brown retired as Camp Ranger of Champlin. Clem Gormley, one of the rangers at Yawgoog, was chosen to take Paul's place at Champlin. Lucy Ciccarelli, Council Registrar, retired in April after 30 years of service to Narragansett Council. Al Gunther, head ranger at Yawgoog, retired on March 31st after 36 years of service at Yawgoog.

The first Urban Scouting Meeting was held in April of 1995. New composting toilets were installed at Yawgoog.

The purchase of the Mellor Land at Buck Hill was completed which would provide for a direct entrance and exit to the proposed Cub Camp at Buck Hill Scout Reservation.

1996

Yawgoog Scout Reservation was the largest Boy Scout Camp in the entire Northeast Region for the 1996 summer. Over $250,000 in Capital Campaign funding was spent to refurbish the Bucklin Building. In 1996 there were 78 members of the Fleur-de-lis Club.

The first Distinguished Citizens Award Dinner was held on June 12th honoring Senator John H. Chafee and J. Terrence Murray, Chairman and CEO of Fleet Corporation. Paul J. Choquette, Jr. chaired this first Distinguished Citizens Award event and continues to serve as Chairman at the writing of this history.

1997

The name of the Urban Scouting was changed to 'Scout Reach Program'. The Paraprofessional Employment Program was initiated in the Narragansett Council by Executive Board vote.

Field Secretary Francine LaVallee passed away in November after a courageous battle with cancer.

The Grand Opening Celebration of the Feinstein Youth Camp and the July Executive Board meeting took on Monday, July 14th at Feinstein Youth Camp.

Paul J. Choquette, Jr. was appointed as President of the Northeast Region.

1998

Andrew M. Erickson became President of the Narragansett Council and Robert Barnes served as Council Commissioner. The Council began its Direct Mail Campaign.

Polly and Andy Erickson

On December 8th, 1998, the Executive Committee passed a 'Feed the Hungry Resolution' that read: "On behalf of the Narragansett Council Boy Scouts of America, we request the President of the United States and our Congress to end hunger in America. On November 7th and 8th of this year, we conducted our 11th Annual Scouting for Food Program and delivered over 350,000 pounds of food to the Rhode Island Food Bank for distribution to the needy. Over the past eleven years, we have collected over 3.6 million pounds of food through the Scouting for Food Program . . . but this does not even begin to solve the problem. Recent studies show that more than 20 million Americans go hungry at some time every month—in a country as rich as ours, every American should hang their head in shame. We encourage you and all Americans to join with the Boy Scouts of America to 'help other people at all times' by making every effort to help meet the needs of the hungry in all of the United States of America."

The dedication of the John Sisson Shelter at Aquapaug took place on November 15th. John was a young Scout who was killed by a drunk driver while changing a tire for a friend. Scouting also lost a great friend and Scouter with the death of Jacques E. Dubois.

The U.S. Postal Service introduced the new 'Scout Stamp'.

Dedication of the Scout Stamp at the Council Office
on 175 Broad Street, Providence.

1999

Paul Choquette agreed to chair the new Capital Campaign for renovations to 175 Broad Street. The Campaign was slated to run from January to April of 1999.

The new National Computer Program, ScoutNet 2000 was installed. On August 16th, long-time friend and supporter of Scouting in Rhode Island, Major General Leonard Holland passed away.

The BSA changed their rules regarding non-citizens of the United States. The BSA will now allow non-citizens to register with the Boy Scouts of America if they agree to follow the rules and regulations of the BSA and the United States of America.

Thomas J. Sisson was hired as the Director of Camping on May 10th, 1999.

Gus Anthony celebrated his 95th Birthday on March 7th.

Paul J. Choquette, Jr. and Robert A. Sirhal were honored at the National Annual Meeting with the coveted Silver Antelope Award. Scout Executive Lyle K. Antonides retired in December of 1999.

Since those early years of Scouting there have been many benefactors who have supported Scouting in the Narragansett Council in a big way. Not all of the benefactors lent their support through financial means but some have given their time and efforts by donating their services to the Council. There is no way we could list all the benefactors of Scouting over the past hundred years, so here we will just 'highlight' a few.

The Nicholson Administration Building at Cub World was named for Paul and Adelaide Nicholson and the Pease High Adventure Theme building at Cub World was named for Jay and Barbara Pease. Without their help, Cub World would not have been built.

Pease High Seas Adventure at Cub World

1997—The just completed Nicholson Administration Building at Cub World

Adelaide and Paul Nicholson at a BSA Fund Raiser in early 2003

Other long time supporters, financial and otherwise, include Robert and Dot Pease, Paul and Libba Choquette, all the Gilbanes, Andy and Polly Erickson, Jon and Sandy Farnum, the entire Gaebe Family, the Galkin Family, Bob and Mary Shea, Charlie McGovern, Eric Jaikes . . . we could fill this page and many more with names of people who have contributed to the well being of Scouting in the Narragansett Council . . . we are grateful for all our friends and for their unending support and friendship.

2000 to 2011—David S. Anderson, Scout Executive

David S. Anderson, Scout Executive
January 2000 to December 2011

On January 15th, 2000, David S. Anderson became the sixth Scout Executive of the Narragansett Council. Previous to his arrival in the Narragansett Council, Dave served as the Scout Executive of the Five Rivers Council in Horseheads, New York.

The Five Rivers Council serves all or part of nine New York and Pennsylvania counties with an area of 5,500 square miles, more than five times the size of Rhode Island. It operates two full-service Scout Camps and a Council-run Scout Shop at a large regional shopping mall. Under Anderson's leadership the Five Rivers Council more than tripled its net worth from $1.7 million to $5.5 million. Dave Anderson, an Eagle Scout and graduate of the University of Rochester, had also served at local Boy Scout Councils in Forth Worth, TX, Rochester, NY and New York City. When asked what his priorities for the Narragansett Council would be he replied, "To continue to provide a program that builds character in young people and teaches them the skills they will need to be good citizens and family members as adults. We owe it to the youth we serve and their parents to provide a program that achieves these important goals." He also cited the Scout Reach Program and the Learning for Life Program as two initiatives that will be priorities for him.

2000

Maxwell Mays was commissioned to paint a picture of Yawgoog and numbered prints became available at a cost of $500.

Left to right: Andrew M. Erickson, David S. Anderson, Maxwell Mays, Brock Bierman at the signing of the rollout of the Camp Yawgoog Maxwell Mays Prints.

Ian Lilien became Director of Field Service on March 15th. At the Annual Meeting in January, Robert H. "Jay" Pease, Jr., took over the reins as President.

Marc Cardin was hired as the new Council Stores Manager.

The new Cope Course at Yawgoog with 26 different elements and two towers was dedicated on July 15th, 2000 in honor of Scouts who served, and continue to serve, in the armed forces. One week's attendance at Yawgoog cost $184.

The 'Trail Signs' newsletter was redesigned and increased use of e-mail for communicating to our members was instituted. The United Way of Southeastern New England adopted an 'inclusion' policy that effectively excluded the Narragansett Council from United Way funding. This action was taken in response to the United States Supreme Court's affirmation of the Boy Scouts of America's right to determine its own membership standards. Newly developed Youth Protection Guidelines were developed and training sessions began throughout the Council.

Narragansett Council conducted '90,000 Hours of Service' for Scouts and Scouters in 2000. Providence Troop 1 held a '90th Anniversary Celebration' of the troop.

Narragansett Council ended the year with 22,251 youth members.

2001

The H. Cushman Anthony Scholarship Fund was established with a $15,000 anonymous donation. This fund was established in Gus' honor with three scholarships to be given each year to deserving Yawgoog staffmen.

At the March Executive Committee Meeting, the proposed Plan for Merger with the Moby Dick Council was voted on and approved to be effective July 1, 2001. With the merger, the 'new' Narragansett Council includes eight major pieces of property, 127,000 total available youth, 25,361 youth members, two full time resident camps and a summer payroll of 260 employees.

Five Mile Pond at Camp Cachalot

Rowing on File Mile Pond

Prescott Dining Hall

Silver Fox Trading Post at Cachalot

Narragansett Council merged with the Moby Dick Council on July 1, 2001. Below is a brief history of the Moby Dick Council.

HISTORY OF THE MOBY DICK COUNCIL

In 1916, the first organized Scouting charters were granted to the Fall River and Fairhaven-New Bedford Councils. These charters would provide area youth in 17 communities throughout Newport, Bristol and Plymouth counties, with the leadership, inspiration, moral and physical fitness of their forefathers.

By 1935, well underway to development, Massachusetts laws required both councils to recharter under the articles of Incorporation. In doing so, the Fairhaven-New Bedford Council rechartered as the Cachalot Council incorporating the towns of Wareham, Marion, Freetown, Rochester, Mattapoisett, Dartmouth and Acushnet. The Fall River council also rechartered as the Massasoit Council providing Scouting leadership to Somerset, Swansea, Westport, Tiverton and Little Compton. Both Councils continued to grow until 1972. Now known as the Cachalot Council and the Massasoit Council, the Councils once again united to form a greater development known as the Moby Dick Council, Boy Scouts of America.

The philosophy behind this merger was a result of awareness of the changing times within each of the Councils' communities. Such a Scouting consolidation would provide the capacity needed to better serve their communities.

For 29 years the Cachalot Council utilized the local Fairhaven-New Bedford Boys' Club facilities of Camp Maxim. In 1945, the Cachalot Executive Board conducted a fund-raiser to purchase and construct Camp Cachalot, meaning "white whale" in Carver, Massachusetts.

Camping for the Fall River Council began in 1917 at Camp Stanford in Fall River, MA and provided an outlet for boys for four years. It was decided in 1921, at a Fall River Council Executive Board meeting, that the purchase of a 100 acre wooded area would take place, naming it Camp Noquochoke. Camp Noquochoke purchased additional acreage in its later years covering over 110 acres on the eastern shore of the Westport River in Westport, MA. Camp Noquochoke continued to serve area youth until 1980.

Camp Cachalot has been maintained and improved since 1954 through community volunteers and grants from the Magee Foundation, local unions and service clubs. Due to this community involvement, Camp Cachalot celebrated its 50th Anniversary in 1996 with a Council wide Camporee. This anniversary, attended by over 500 Scouts and Scouting Alumni, bore witness to Camp Cachalot's ability to bring alive The Scouting Handbook to more than 30,000 over 50 years.

As the Moby Dick Council grew, so did their communities. A new era developed in the late 80's and early 90's. Drugs and hunger plagued the Moby Dick Council's families, friends and community at large. Rather than sit back and watch their communities deteriorate, the Moby Dick Council joined forces in a nationwide "Good Turns" program which involved Donor Awareness, Drugs A Deadly Game and Scouting for Food. The project developed nationally supplementing the traditional physical and mental fitness programs involving 2,400 Scouts and Explorers of the Moby Dick Council. The individual programs provided awareness for the need for organ donors, drug prevention, and the collection of more than a quarter of a million food items for local food pantries in the Massachusetts South Coast area.

Such selfless acts and community projects merited the Moby Dick Council the National Quality Council Award by the Boy Scouts of America in 1996.

Today, the Moby Dick Council serves approximately 3,900 youth and members ranging in ages of Cub Scout 7 to 12, Boy Scout 11 to 18 and teenage men and women in the Exploring Program. Over 700 volunteer leaders serving in varied capacities are responsible for implementing the Scouting Programs throughout the 17 communities served by the Council.

The mission of the Moby Dick Council stood through its religious, civic, fraternal, corporate and community organizations working in a partnership to provide Scouting to the youth of its communities. In doing so, the Council received 24% of its operating budget support from the United Way of Fall River and New Bedford. The financial support extended through its Friends of Scouting Annual Campaign effort and from special events. For 25 years, the Moby Dick Council grew to become an effective program throughout its community. From the boys who participate to the communities they serve, the Moby Dick Council, Boy Scouts of America truly honored their pledge and oath.

While still providing a quality program to the youth of Massachusetts, the Moby Dick Council began to fall on hard times. In 1999, the Scout Executive became ill and was unable to return to work. It became increasingly harder to serve the youth of Massachusetts and on July 1, 2001, the Moby Dick Council (#245) in New Bedford, Massachusetts, merged with the Narragansett Council (#546) adding 17 more cities and towns in Massachusetts to the 6 cities and towns the Narragansett Council was already serving.

Along with the merger with Moby Dick Council came the acquisition of the Cachalot Scout Reservation—History of Cachalot Scout Reservation

On May 13th, 1935, as part of complying with new rules of incorporation for Boy Scout councils in Massachusetts, the New Bedford Council changed its name to the Cachalot Council. The name, derived from the French and Portuguese words for sperm whale, was proposed by Joe Allen, of the [Martha's] Vineyard Gazette, in January of 1933 to honor the history of whaling in New Bedford.

At the time, the Council did own a property that was used as a camp. This property, off Rock O' Dundee Road in South Dartmouth, was too small and lacked adequate water sources, both for drinking and swimming. For a short time, from 1937 through 1942, the council shared the summer camp facilities of the Fall River Council, but this was deemed "not satisfactory for many reasons." From 1943 through 1945, summer camp was held at Camp Maxim, which was owned by the local Boys Club, and also failed to meet the needs of the program.

In 1945, the Cachalot Council conducted a capital fundraising campaign expressly for the purpose of acquiring a suitable camp. Many local businesses and individuals contributed, and the campaign successfully raised $75,000. At the same time, the council began looking for a suitable property. After considering several properties, they placed on offer on a large parcel adjacent to the southeastern corner of Myles Standish State Forest, owned by "The Five Mile Corporation." This corporation, headed by Theodore Steinway (of Steinway & Sons Piano), Albert Hathaway, and Russell Davis, had purchased the property during the Great Depression for a mere $12,000, and agreed to sell it to the council for the same price. The deed was signed over in January 1946, and preparations immediately commenced to open the Camp for its first summer camp season ever, with Roland Deneault as Camp Director, in summer of the same year. It has operated continuously since.

During its first few years of operation, the Camp saw a flurry of activity, moving or constructing buildings, and otherwise preparing the property for use as a year-round Boy Scout camping facility. The 21 Club was moved to Cachalot from its original site by Drift Road in Westport in or before 1948, and one of its earliest uses in camp was as the trading post. An administration building (the current Phillips House and a Quonset hut (serving as a maintenance building and storage) were constructed, along with an open waterfront tower (in 1950) and swimming docks.

The first large building to open in Camp was the Dining Hall, which was completed and first used during summer camp in 1951. Prior to the construction of a permanent dining hall, meals were prepared and served under a large military-style tent with a floor platform sitting on the same site as the Dining Hall (early camp reports mention having to coat the wooden floor with creosote at the start of each season!) The Dining Hall at this point had no fireplace, and consisted only of most what is now the dining room area.

Construction at Camp continued into the early 1960s, seeing a Ranger's Cabin (converted from an old latrine—there were no resident rangers just yet) built; a fireplace added to the 21 Club; the "Tom Cullen Memorial Archway" erected, all in the early 50s; and a Cook's Cabin, the old shower house, a rifle range, and the Boat House built in 1960.

The last bit of planned construction for the early 1960s was for a new Trading Post, the foundation of which was completed in early May, 1964, with framing to commence on May 22nd, 1964. Unfortunately, fate had something else in mind for that weekend.

One of the most significant events in Cachalot's history took place on the weekend of May 22nd, 1964, during the spring Camp-o-ree. During that spring Camp-o-ree, however, fire swept into Cachalot from the adjoining Myles Standish State Forest, burning through Cachalot, eventually threatening homes in Plymouth and Wareham, and stopping only when it reached White Island Pond to the east, on May 24th, 1964. In all, 5,500 acres of forest, including most of Cachalot, were consumed by the blaze. Over 700 Scouts and Scouters were evacuated from Cachalot, but fortunately there were no significant injuries at Camp. Most of the major buildings on the property were spared—but the Quonset Hut (which exploded when the gasoline stored inside ignited), a commissary building, the original Cook's Cabin, and the outpost shelter at Abner's Pond were lost, along with all of the tent site latrines. The New Bedford Standard-Times later reported that the fire was the work of an arsonist who had set no fewer than 63 separate blazes. Most of these were lit by improvised incendiary devices comprised of a lit cigarette and pack of matches affixed to rocks with tape and thrown into the forest.

Rebuilding of the property began immediately, but many troops that summer attended neighboring Camp Squanto in cooperation with the Squanto Council. An outpost camp would be operated at Cachalot for interested troops as well. This arrangement continued through the summer of 1965, with Cachalot's own Sumner Morse running the joint program in its second year. Despite the fire, Cachalot had remained open throughout those first two years of recovery, even hosting a reduced summer camp program.

In 1966, the summer camp program at Cachalot resumed full operation.

In late May of 1967, in an effort to emphasize that Cachalot was more than just a summer camp and that it was in fact a year-round training center for the

Council, it was suggested by Kenneth Liberty, then the Scout Executive, to change the name of the property. The new name, recommended by the Camping and Properties Committee, and approved by the Executive Board, would be "Cachalot Council Scout Reservation. The concern was that many potential donors would be more willing to give to a year round reservation than to something that operated only a few weeks each summer.

After the fire, the Cook's Cabin as it exists today was constructed, a new Waterfront Tower was erected in 1965, and by 1966, the Dining Hall had also undergone a major expansion, adding more seating area on the end facing the Cook's Cabin, and a large new kitchen area, almost doubling the footprint of the building. The duplex building and maintenance building were added soon after. 1968 saw the construction and dedication of the Raymond F. Covill Memorial Chapel, 1969 the construction of the Ranger's Residence, and Cachalot's first full-time, resident ranger, Armand Guilmette. This was followed by another flurry of activity in the early 1970s which saw the 21 Club winterized with funding from the Standard-Times, the Adirondack shelters built, and the first Council Ring on the current site established.

In order to control the water rights and right-of-way to Five Mile Pond, the cranberry bogs at the southern end of Camp (and the only piece extending into Wareham) were purchased from their previous owner, Richard Arne Johnson of South Carver, in 1971. This added another 40 acres to the property.

In 1972, a merger of the Fall River-centered Massasoit Council with the New Bedford-based Cachalot Council took place, forming the new Moby Dick Council. It served youth from Tiverton, RI and Somerset in the west to Wareham in the east.

From 1972 through 1977, the Moby Dick Council continued to operate program at both of the camps it now owned, Camp Noquochoke in Westport and Camp Cachalot in Plymouth. In the Fall of 1977, due to financial reasons, the Executive Board made the decision to sell the Camp Cachalot property. Volunteers, in an attempt to keep Cachalot as a Scout camp, worked to find a way to avoid the selling of the property in a campaign that postponed any talk of the sale until June, 1978. A task force was put together, and the decision was made to sell the smaller Noquochoke facility.

Noquochoke ceased operation in 1978 and was sold by 1980.

Two new cabins were constructed and opened for use at Cachalot in 1980. Flush toilets with real septic systems were constructed in James West (Site 7), Baden-Powell (Site 8), and between Acooshnet (Site 1) and Sippican (Site 2).

Beginning at its 1983 Ordeal Weekend, the Neemat Lodge set out on what would be its largest, longest single service project—an effort to restore and improve the Council Ring. This would take two years of effort, mostly in the form of monthly work weekends, and involved completely tearing down the old structures, elevating the stage by moving large quantities of sand, cutting a new, less steep (and less likely to erode) approach path, planting new trees on the old approach, and terracing and building new seating. With the exception of some tree and telephone pole cutting, done by chainsaw, this was done entirely by hand and predominantly by the youth of the lodge.

Throughout the 1980s, many units in the Council also contributed to an effort to reforest many areas of Camp. In addition to the lingering effects of the 1964 fire, many of the pitch pines in camp were infested, and in many cases killed by, an insect called an Eastern, or Pitch Pine Looper. Large areas along the main road and behind the Adirondacks were cleared with a bulldozer and brush cutter, and were replanted with pine saplings. These were mostly white pine and not native pitch pine, and the re-plantings have grown with mixed success.

The Health Lodge was expanded, its size nearly doubling, in 1985, with the addition of a wing specifically for the Camp Nurse's residence. This allowed the whole of the original building to be used strictly as the medical facility, for checkups and for treatment or quarantine of sick campers during summer camp. The 21 Club also underwent major revisions at this time, with all of its windows being replaced, the interior re-insulated and re-paneled, the exterior re-sided, and a new, fully-covered porch built on the front of the building.

In 1987, the Trading Post was completely destroyed by a nighttime fire. Fortunately, the fire had been contained to the site of the building itself, and a larger conflagration had been avoided. It would take well over a year, with the camp Commissioner's Corner building returning to its original role as the Trading Post in the interim, but a new slab was poured and a new, concrete block building would be erected on the same site to take its place.

Numerous other small fires occurred in and around Cachalot though the 1980s and 1990s, including a large fire at Charge Pond whose smoke plume was clearly visible in Camp from the waterfront, during the Sunday swimmers tests during summer camp. Small areas near Little Long Pond, on the trail to Stumpy Pond, and in the staff site itself also burned, but were extinguished quickly and caused no lasting damage. The first two were the result of abandoned, possibly stolen vehicles being set ablaze; the last was caused by an electrical problem.

The 1980s also saw some of the busiest summer seasons in Cachalot's history, with as many as 9 weeks of program each summer, encompassing a "staff week", 4 weeks of Boy Scout overnight camp, 3-4 weeks of Cub Day Camp, and, for several years, a week of Webelos overnight camp. These weeks were, if not at capacity, very well attended, to the point of eating in shifts in the dining hall one or two weeks a summer.

Small construction projects dominated the 1990s. These included more modern bathrooms and showers being built in the sites that did not yet have them, the expansion of the rifle range to include a shotgun range, another small addition and new walk-in cooler for the Dining Hall, and a shelter for the archery range. The docks at the waterfront were also replaced twice, with the current set meant to be left in over the winter months and able to withstand ice on Five Mile Pond.

The waterfront changed more dramatically in 1998, with the construction of a new lookout tower to replace the deteriorating Andrew Jackson Memorial Waterfront Tower. The new tower, designed to incorporate not only storage but also be the residence of members of the Aquatics staff, was set much further back from the water's edge. As a result of this change, and the addition of additional fencing, the usable beach area of the waterfront has been significantly increased.

In May of 1995, together with two of neighboring councils Annawon and Cape Cod and_the Islands Councils), the Moby Dick Council formed a group known as the Southeastern Massachusetts Camping Alliance, or SEMCA. Under this umbrella organization, Cachalot became the Boy Scout-level summer camp for all three councils, helping to ensure attendance at the camp. Cub Scouts and Webelos would attend programs at Camp Norse, Annawon's camp, and Cape Cod and the Island's Camp Greenough was designated as an "adventure outpost" camp for older Scouts.

In 1997, the council was approached by the State of Massachusetts to establish a "conservation restriction" on the outer, undeveloped portions of Cachalot. Effectively, the council would grant a permanent lease to the state, and agree not to develop specific areas in camp, in exchange for the state handling all forest and wildlife management in that area and providing access to the public for hunting and fishing. It would also be a financial windfall for the Council, with the state paying the council one million dollars for this lease. A new Wildlife Management Area was established in 1998.

In 2002, Moby Dick Council's Scout Executive, Gerald Monahan, retired. It was at this point that the Council was informed that no new executive would be hired to replace him, and without a Scout Executive no charter for the Council could be issued. Soon after, Narragansett Council approached the Moby Dick Executive Board with an offer to merge, keeping the two existing districts as districts of the merged Council, and maintaining Cachalot as a property of the new Council. The Board accepted, and the Moby Dick Council ceased to be, with final approval coming with an act of the Massachusetts State Legislature in September of 2003. Richard F. Partridge was President of the Moby Dick Council at the time of the merger and now serves on the Narragansett Council Executive Board.

Recent construction in Camp includes a set of 3-season cabins built mainly to house the summer camp staff, dubbed "Magee Village", the addition of a shower facility on the back side of the Trading Post, and the siding of the Trading Post in rough-edged wood siding to better fit in with other buildings in Camp. Work also continues on completing the build-out of modern shower and latrine facilities in all of the summer camp sites, with the most recent addition being made in 2005.

Fishing and Sailing on Five Mile Pond at Cachalot

2001 (Continued)

The Three Point Kitchen at Camp Yawgoog was refurbished at a cost of $115,000. The Town of Burrillville purchased the land-locked piece of property in Burrillville (66.5 acres) known as the 'Mossberg Property' for a sum of $22,500.

2001—Paul and Libba Choquette when Paul received the Distinguished Citizens Award with Eagle Scout Erik Kandler from Troop 138 West Kingston

The Providence and Skeleton Valley Districts were merged and given the new name of 'Netop' District. The Scouting for Food Drive resulted in a record 344,710 pounds of food collected. Narragansett Council earned the Quality Council Award.

2002

Onsite-Insight performed a physical needs assessment for Yawgoog, Buck Hill, Cub World and Champlin at a cost of $20,000. A new roof was put on the Cachalot Dining Hall and a new porch was constructed, in addition to a new tile floor in the kitchen. The building of the Buxton Shelter was completed in April.

Andy Erickson revitalized the Planned Giving Committee adding two new levels of giving: The John R. Rathom Club ($5,000 and over) and The J. Harold Williams Club ($10,000 and over).

A contract was signed with the Alhambra Building Company to build the Yawgoog Museum at an approximate cost of $154,000.

Lot 53 in Burrillville was sold for the sum of $15,000 and deposited into the Endowment Funds of the Rhode Island Boy Scouts. The Rhode Island Boy Scouts approved the sale of a conservation easement with the Nature Conservancy for the Sandsland Property in Block Island. The Rhode Island Boy Scouts continue to own the property and the easement allowed continued use of the property as before, allowed for the relocation of campsites, for the construction of a restroom facility if necessary and prohibit public access. The only change was that RIBS no longer has the right to commercially develop the property and gave the Nature Conservancy the right to manage the plant and animal species on the property. The Nature Conservancy paid the Rhode Island Boy Scouts $1.1 million for the easement which was added to the RIBS Endowment Funds. The Rhode Island Boy Scouts also approved the sale of two parcels in Little Compton (Lots 11 and 14) to the Little Compton Agricultural Land Trust. The Council accepted a donation of a 3.5 acre parcel of land along the Palmer River adjacent to Camp Buxton. The land is fairly wet but will serve as a buffer at Camp Buxton.

Joe Gencarella served as the Chair of the 2003-2007 Strategic Plan. 240 Scouts attended an All Faith Camporee at Yawgoog in September.

The Council ended the year with 25,520 young people in 543 Cub Scout Packs, Boy Scout Troops, Venture Crews, Explorer Posts and Learning for Life Groups. The Narragansett Council had 251 Eagle Scouts in the Class of 2002.

2003

The 2003 Camp Fees to attend Yawgoog were at $230 for an in-council Scout and $245 for an out-of-council Scout.

The State of Massachusetts passed new legislation requiring background checks on all current and prospective volunteers in youth serving organizations. The Massachusetts Criminal Records Board approved the Council's application for access to CORI records and the Council began processing background checks on all adult volunteer leaders to comply with the relevant Massachusetts legislation.

Refurbishment of the Medicine Bow Kitchen was completed at Yawgoog. The new Trading Post and YAA Heritage Center was also completed and ready for the first week of summer camp. Marc Andreo was hired to serve the Council as its new Director of Field Service replacing Ian Lilien who was promoted to Scout Executive of the Pikes Peak Council in Colorado Springs, CO.

A Service Center Relocation Committee was formed under the guidance of Past President Jay Pease to discuss the options of selling the Broad Street Office and relocating the Council Offices. The legal issue preventing the final approval of the merger of the Moby Dick Council and the Narragansett Council was resolved and the restated articles of merger were approved by the Massachusetts Secretary of State.

1,400 participants took part in the 2003 Council Camporee. The East Bay Scout Shop was moved from New Bedford to the Swansea Mall which allowed the Council to reach more Scouters in a centrally located area.

Barbara and Jay Pease at the 2003 Council Recognition Dinner

2004

The Scout Store at 175 Broad Street was closed on January 15th and the West Bay Scout Shop at Summit Square Plaza on Route 2 in Warwick opened its doors on February 1st.

The Council spent $90,000 to bring the three dining halls at Yawgoog in compliance with the fire code.

The Narragansett Council is the 40th largest council in a total of 315 councils throughout the United States.

The Rhode Island Boy Scouts sold 175 Broad Street for $1.9 million and the Narragansett Council negotiated a lease for space at 10 Risho Avenue in East Providence for five years. From the sale of the building, $1.7 million was deposited into the Endowment Funds of the Rhode Island Boy Scouts and the remaining $200,000 was used to complete the move to Risho Avenue. The Council Office was up and running at 10 Risho Avenue on October 15th. The two murals hanging at 175 Broad Street were removed. The mural in the lobby of Broad Street painted by Carl Ritman was hung at "The Barn" (the old warehouse) at Yawgoog and is on display there as of the writing of this history. The Barn is used for Farm Mechanics and Farming Merit Badges. The mural that was located in the Board Room is on loan and is hung at Benefit Concepts, 20 Risho Avenue, East Providence. John and Jay Hoder were kind enough to offer their space to hang the mural until a permanent home can be found.

The Cachalot Alumni Association was formed and Camp Cachalot celebrated its first Alumni gathering in 2004. Participation in the COPE Program grew to 4,100 students in 2004 and the fee revenue was up by more than 50%. A new Wild West Theme area was opened at Cub World

2005

The Rhode Island Boy Scouts dissolved the Yawgoog Fire Department as the corporation no longer served any purpose as the camp is well served by the Hopkinton Fire Department.

The Executive Board adopted a resolution requiring that "direct contact" leaders (Scoutmasters, Assistant Scoutmasters, Cubmasters and Den Leaders) be trained as a requirement in order to charter a unit in 2007. Any exception to this rule would have to be approved by the Council Key 3.

The Executive Board voted to merge the Blackstone Valley District with the Thundermist District and the new name became Thunder Valley District.

In 1937 a 2.1 acre parcel of beach land was deeded to the Cachalot Council for use exclusively by the Siasconset Troop of the BSA. Since the troop no longer existed, the Executive Committee voted to transfer Narragansett Council's interest in the property to the Cape & Islands Council for a sum of $25,000.

A pre-fabricated building (Warehouse) was erected at the end of the parking lot by the shop at Yawgoog. The Council retained Pare Engineering in the first step to develop a new waste disposal system at Yawgoog.

In an attempt to have better access to the National Scout Net System, the office hours at the Council Service Center were changed from 9 to 5 to 8 a.m. to 4 p.m.

Camp Yawgoog closed for two weeks on July 26th as the Norovirus worked its way through Rhode Island. After consultation with the Health Department and a total disinfecting of the entire camp, Yawgoog reopened on August 7th for the 7th and 8th weeks of summer camp.

2006

The Rhode Island Boy Scouts purchased the Ross Property at a sum of $230,000. The Rhode Island Boy Scouts had been leasing this 200 acres parcel at Buck Hill which surrounded three sides of their property. The lease gave the Council the option to purchase this acreage at market value upon the death of Arthur Ross.

Executive Board Member George Shuster led the charge in the first 'Gathering of Lost Eagles' in May of 2006 at the Squantum Association with 82 people in attendance. Internet rechartering was introduced in Narragansett Council.

The first phase of the Yawgoog ISDS System was instituted after the close of camp. The first phase included the conversion of the Medicine Bow Latrines to flush toilets using the excess capacity in the Sandy Beach leach field.

The East Bay Scout Shop moved from its location at the Swansea Mall to 79 Swansea Mall Drive.

A pilot program was instituted at Camp Buxton for the Massachusetts Diabetes Association in Fall River to run a camp for children with diabetes. The program is still in effect at this writing.

Day Camp attendance was up by 11% to the highest level in four years.

2007

Phase Two of the Yawgoog ISDS System was designed by Pare Engineering which included the conversion of the latrines in Three Point to flush toilets and the construction of a new leach field in Anthony Acres. A new Latrine/Shower House was completed at Cachalot and a new Maintenance Building was added at Cub World.

A joint Camping venture was developed with the Mohegan, Annawon and Cape & Islands Council for use of Narragansett Council's Camp Cachalot and Cub World.

Marc Andreo was selected as the Scout Executive to Westchester-Putnam Council and left the Council's employ in March. Jim Waters, a New Englander and an Eagle Scout, was hired as the new Director of Field Service.

The Family Campground Program at Buck Hill was phased out in October of 2007. Camp Buxton was shut down for a short time as 1,600 red pine trees were infected with insects and were dead. The trees were cut down and removed.

A field service realignment was completed and the 1910 District was born primarily serving the Hispanic communities in urban areas.

The Council raised over $1,000,000 for the first time and the new Webelos resident camp program was back at Yawgoog in 2007.

2008

The Distinguished Commissioner's Award was developed with the Bronze Award for Unit Commissioners, the Gold Award for volunteers on the District level and the Silver Award for volunteers on the Council level. Arthur W. Keegan was the first to receive the Silver Distinguished Commissioner's Award.

On Easter Sunday evening the Rotary Shelter at Camp Champlin was destroyed by fire. The Cranston Fire Marshall determined that it was arson. With the closing of the Family Campground at Buck Hill, the Rhode Island Boy Scouts identified several excess parcels of land totaling about 220 acres. These parcels, which are not part of the core holdings around Wakefield Pond, include the Croff Road ranger's house with shop and pole barn; Cabin in the Pines; School House; two vacant lots on the west side of Croff Road; 180 acres East of Croff Road and North of Wakefield Pond.

The Order of the Arrow conducted a work weekend at Camp Buxton planting trees to replace the red pines that died of disease. Funds from the Magee Trust were used to clear the brush and trees from the power lines and replace some of the poles that carry the mile long line into Camp Cachalot. A new roof was placed on the Handicraft Lodge at Cachalot. Phase II of the Yawgoog ISDS project was completed and the permit application for Phase III which includes the Sandy Beach latrines and the Medicine Bow Kitchen was submitted.

The Narragansett Council celebrated its 10th year of the International Exchange Program with the Dominican Republic.

2009

New docks were installed at the new waterfront at Cub World and a number of projects including removal of an old climbing wall and general clean up were completed by the Order of the Arrow. The Protestant Committee on Scouting raised money and renovated the Four Eagles Cabin which included a new kitchen and bathroom. The Cachalot Alumni Association replaced half of the benches in the Chapel as well as completing other significant projects at Camp Cachalot. Phase III of the Yawgoog ISDS project was completed. Every site has flush toilets and all of the dining halls are tied into the new system. The Hamilton Lodge at Buck Hill was renovated for use by Scouts. Renovations included reconfiguration of the Lodge to include two bunk rooms, two rooms for adults, two bathrooms and a new kitchen and great room. New electrical and new plumbing was put throughout the Lodge.

Narragansett Council revised its 100% Trained Leader Policy no longer making it a requirement for rechartering.

2010

The Boy Scouts of America is celebrating the 100th Anniversary of Scouting this year as is the Rhode Island Boy Scouts. A special website featuring 100 recent Eagle Scouts went live in February.

The four Regional Offices were closed as January 1st, 2010 and operations were moved to the National Office in Texas. Andrew C. Hewitt was elected Council President at the Annual Meeting in January.

A Structure Task Force was developed to review what the Council needs to do to adapt to the changes in society. At the July Executive Board Meeting, Board Members voted to approve the new council structure and to (1) eliminate the current geographic boundaries known as districts and the associated structure; and (2) effective September 1st, to provide service and support at the council level directly to local communities. In addition it was voted to eliminate the positions of

Vice President for District Operations and the position of Vice President/Nominating Committee Chair and to nominate Fr. Angelo Carusi and Lee Alan Duckworth to the newly created positions of Service Area Vice Presidents.

At a Special Meeting of the Rhode Island Boy Scouts on September 30th, the sale of 203 Croff Road for $150,000 was voted on and approved. The Asset Management Committee authorized the Scout Executive to make arrangements to have the two structures demolished. Also, the sale of the 180 acre parcel at Buck Hill to the Rhode Island Department of Environmental Management is still pending and the closing date was extended to December 31st, 2010.

Highlighted History of BSA
and Yawgoog Scout Reservation

1907-1909

- 1907 British Lord Robert S. S. Baden-Powell organizes the first Boy Scout Camp on Brownsea Island, off the coast of England, starting the Scouting movement.
- 1908 Lord S. S. Robert Baden-Powell publishes "Scouting for Boys"
- 1900 Chicago publisher William D. Boyce lost his way in a dense London fog. A boy came to his aid and, after guiding the man, refused a tip, explaining that as a Scout he would not take a tip for doing a Good Turn. This gesture by an unknown Scout inspired a meeting with Robert Baden-Powell.

1910-1919

- 1910 Baden-Powell's Scout movement takes root in America and Rhode Island.
- Following his visit with Baden Powell William Boyce incorporated the Boy Scouts of America in the District of Columbia, February 8th. Rhode Island State Scout Committee formed on September 6.
- 1911 Rhode Island Boy Scouts chartered as a State corporation on April 13th, 1911. 18-year old Scout Joseph Lane of Providence, RI, joins George S. Barton, of Somerville, Mass., as one of four editors of a new youth magazine called "Boy's Life".
- 1912 "Boy's Life" moves to Providence, RI with a circulation of ~65,000. Magazine is sold to the Boy Scouts of America.
- 1916 RI Boy Scouts open Yawgoog's first camp season. Donald North is Camp Director at the rocky site of the uninhabited 130 acre Palmer Farm on the shores of Yawgoog Pond, about 250 Scouts attend.
- BSA chartered by Congress, June 15th US Code, Title 36, Section 21, ch. 148, Sec. 1, 39 Stat. 227—to provide an educational program for boys and young adults to build character, to train in the responsibilities of participating citizenship, and to develop personal fitness.
- 1917 Rhode Island Boy Scouts merged with w:Boy Scouts of America as Greater Providence Council. Tents moved from rocky meadow, now Tim O'Neil Field, to old orchard, near present Ranger's parking lot.
- 1919 J. Harold Williams serves his first of 43 years as camp Chief. The old Palmer barn becomes the Opry House for camp shows. First camp dining hall, now Reservation trading post, built.

1920-1929

- 1920 Weekly visits by His Regalness, the "King of Yawgoog," result in establishment of the "Knights of Yawgoog," a camp honor society for adult leaders

- 1921 H. Cushman "Gus" Anthony joins Yawgoog staff as a "Junior Officer" responsible for "Sinks, Incinerators and Wash Stands". "Clean it or burn it".
- 1922 Dress Parade instituted by West Point cadet Leslie Fletcher.
- 1923 All summer camp at campsites Tuocs and Oak Ridge established.
- 1924 Camp divided between "Upper Camp" and "Lower Camp;" Bucklin Lodge, now Sharpe Lodge, also known as the Three Point Dining Hall, built.
- 1925 King Phillips Island purchased.
- 1926 Scout Mother's Hospital, presently Three Point Director cabin, built.
- 1927 "Yawgoog Daily News" (1927-35) and tradition of weekly themes begin. T. Dawson Brown arranges purchase of land for Camp Sandy Beach. Dan Lamb presents Chief Williams with charred remains of hand-hewn bow intended for him—"good medicine".
- 1928 Colonel G. Edward Buxton, co-founder of Rhode Island Scouting, declares Yawgoog "A Scout Adventureland forever" during dedication of Sandy Beach area. Camp Sandy Beach opened for camping that summer will all-summer pioneer "tepee" camp.
- 1929 Yawgoog's third dining hall, Rathom's Lodge, built and Camp Medicine Bow division established alongside the Camp Three Point division. The Yawgoog Daily News regards the dedication "of supreme importance to every boy who would die with the cry of 'Yawgoog' on his lips.". Saturday Night Shows are held this summer.

1930-1939

- 1930 Yawgoog devastated by forest fire on May 4, 5, 6. Reforestation begins immediately. Narragansett Council, BSA #546, formed when the Greater Providence Council merged with three other councils in Newport, Pawtucket-Central Falls, and Woonsocket. First "Stockade" (handicraft area) built. Two navy "pulling cutters" added to Yawgoog fleet.
- 1931 The Bucklin area buildings dedicated on the Fourth of July.
- 1932 Fort Hilton Trading Post established on Hill 407. Scouts can have 25 cents credit as they hike the Yawgoog trails.
- 1933 Yawgoog's famous "Slade's Bridge" spans "The Gut" between King Phillips Island and the mainland—a great attraction until closed in 1946.
- 1935 Curtis Tract purchased
- 1936 Ranger's house built for Inky Armstrong family.
- 1937 Fort Hilton hike program discontinued; 2,793 Scouts attended camp; first BSA National Scout Jamboree held in Washington, DC; Rhode Island Scouts participated in this and every jamboree since.
- 1938 Following the camp season the "Big Hurricane" of 1938 blew down many trees that had survived the fire of 1930; the lumber from these toppled trees helped build Jesse H. Metcalf Lodge.
- 1939 Jesse H. Metcalf Lodge, dining hall for Sandy Beach Division, dedicated.

1940-1949

- 1940 22nd annual performance of Barum and Bayrum's Circus held at Bucklin Memorial
- 1941 January 8th, world Scouting founder and Chief Scout of the World, Baden-Powell died at age 83 years; Armington Memorial Health Lodge built at Yawgoog
- 1942 Senator and Mrs. Jesse H. Metcalf pay the bill for completion of camp water system
- 1943 America at War, many former Yawgoog staff answer call to serve; Memorial Bell Tower at Three Point dedicated in remembrance of "Scouts who died for God and country;" tradition of respectful silence during its noontime tolling develops.
- 1944 Growing pains result in opening of three new campsites: Weemat, Pioneer, and Lewis & Clark). Yawgoog hires first resident Registered Nurse.
- 1946 J. Harold Williams Amphitheater dedicated; Saturday Shows and important ceremonies take place there; Dress Parade field named after Scout Commissioner Tim O'Neil.
- 1947 "The Geologic Story of Camp Yawgoog," by Eagle Scout and geologist Gerry Richmond, published.
- 1948 Allan and Stuart Halladay introduce "Chief Yawgoog" totem; "This is Yawgoog," an inspiring "amphitheater spectacle," performed three times to rave reviews
- 1949 A new and bigger frontier "Stockade" for handicrafts and camp lore constructed with help from Town Criers and Providence Rotary Club

1950-1959

- 1950 John "Johnny Appleseed" Page creates "Totin' Chip" program at Yawgoog; Worship centers for Catholic, Jewish, and Protestant faiths completed; second BSA National Scout Jamboree held in Valley Forge, PA, Chief Williams helped run the jamboree
- 1951 "Gus" Anthony assumes role as Camp Director as "Chief" Williams presents his pageant "American Days" at World Jamboree; Chief Yawgoog patch with segments established
- 1952 Benefit swims start; Yawgoog on cover of Boys Life
- 1953 Water rights to Yawgoog and Wincheck Ponds secured through efforts of T. Dawson Brown; third BSA National Scout Jamboree held in Irvine Ranch, CA
- 1954 "Adventure Trails" program, featuring overnighters to backwoods skill centers, begins; the first international Scouts at Yawgoog result in show, "A Bridge Across the World"
- 1955 Yawgoog's 40th season; visiting Israeli Scouts and leaders write that at Yawgoog they found "the true brotherhood of Scouts"

- 1956 Apprentice-in-Training program begins (precursor to present day CIT program); memorial to beloved Yawgoog leader, Angelo Zuccolo
- 1957 Workshop and storehouse built; Adams gateway to Protestant Cathedral dedicated; 4th BSA National Scout Jamboree held in Valley Forge, PA, Chief Williams runs big show
- 1958 Over 1,000 campers during the first week in July; outpost camping really booming!; Wincheck Tribe of Indians becomes Wincheck Lodge, Order of the Arrow; Yawgoog's first Ranger Inky Armstrong retired
- Albert Gunther becomes Yawgoog's second Ranger and Fire Chief, moves into Camp Ranger house with his wife Dianne; season's attendance tops 7,000, including 150,000th Scout

1960-1969

- 1960 Annual camp show is "Birthday Party" in honor of Golden Jubilee of Scouting; 5th National Scout "Golden Jubilee" Jamboree attended by RI Scouts in Colorado Springs, CO
- 1961 Yawgoog completely refurbished and enlarged with support from "Golden Jubilee Fund;" totem poles, one honoring Yawgoog's early days, the other, "Chief" Williams, erected; 'Charlie Brown' outboard motor boat donated; water skiing added to camp program
- 1962 "Chief" Williams retires as "Camp Chief;" "Uncle Brad" Field (longtime Director of Medicine Bow), at 80, retires as Camp Factor
- 1963 Camp Commissioner services introduced; resident doctors begin service at camp, thanks to Dr. Melvin Hoffman
- 1964 Patrol method emphasized as "Honor Patrol"; pennants awarded; 6th National Scout Jamboree attended by RI Scouts at Valley Forge, PA
- 1965 Yawgoog celebrates its 50th (Golden Jubilee) camping season; Counselor-in-Training ("CIT") program in full swing
- 1966 "Baden Powell Quality Plus Award" presented to 73 troops; Al Murray's 38th and final official staff season
- 1967 Program aimed at reaching inner city youth begins with 185 non-Scouts attending camp
- 1968 "Gus" Anthony retires as Camp Director after 53 years as camper and staffman; final Saturday Show features reminiscences by Gus's "Model T"
- 1969 Don Fowler, Gus's assistant for 4 years, assumes reins as Director; 7th National Scout Jamboree attended by RI Scouts in Farragut State Park, Idaho

1970-1979

- 1970 "Yawgoog Scout Camps" becomes "Yawgoog Scout Reservation;" the three divisions are called "camps"
- 1971 Phil Tracy becomes Yawgoog Director; "Patrol-Power" program helps promote patrol methods at camp

- The Campmaster Corps was formed at Yawgoog in 1972.
- 1973 First harvesting of white pines planted after 1930 fire; 8th National Scout Jamboree attended by RI Scouts in Moraine State Park, PA
- 1975 King Phillips Wilderness Center ("KPWC"), combining wilderness survival, Indian lore, and nature study, opens on Phillips Island
- 1976 J. Harold Williams Brotherhood Award established in memoriam; the nation's bicentennial celebrated with gala show week 2; a hurricane warning ushers Scouts to dining halls for a "camp-in" late in summer
- 1977 Yawgoog's 250,000th Scout passes through T. Dawson Brown gateway; first planting of Yawgoog Christmas trees; 9th National Scout Jamboree attended by RI Scouts in Moraine State Park, PA
- 1979 International Danish Scout Anders Cosmus Pyndt serves second full year on staff

1980-1989

- 1980 Yawgoog's nature program has a new base in revitalized old Palmer barn; the "Challenge Program," featuring initiative games and "ropes course" activities, begins
- Gus Anthony founds Alumni Association; over 100 out-of-council troops attend camp; 10th National Scout Jamboree attended by RI Scouts at Fort A. P. Hill, Virginia
- 1982 Scouts from different troops form patrols with staff for fun activities in "Operation Friendship"
- 1983 Old Palmer barn is razed; nature center given new solar-paneled home
- 1984 "Handicapped Awareness Trail" ("HAT") established; Black Powder shooting and windsurfing are new programs; Health Lodge refurbished by ranger staff
- 1985 "Project Quest" high adventure program successfully launched; 246 acres added north of "Anthony Acres"; 11th National Scout Jamboree attended by RI Scouts at Fort A. P. Hill, VA
- 1986 Joe Herbold becomes Chair of the Yawgoog Alumni Association; Scouts and staff rescue balloonists on pond
- 1987 Bill Burns serves first year as Yawgoog Director
- 1988 Al Gunther's 30th year as Camp Ranger; devoted Yawgoog Scouter and Alumni Treasurer Donald C. Dewing (over 50 years SM of Troop 82 Prov.) dies; the "H. Cushman Anthony Stockade" dedicated
- 1989 Paul Boisvert becomes Yawgoog's 9th Director; campsite for handicapped Scouts installed at Sandy Beach; crafts pavilions dedicated 12th National Scout Jamboree attended by RI Scouts at Fort A. P. Hill, VA

1990-1999

- 1990 Yawgoog celebrates its 75th camping season
- 1992 Paul Bernetsky becomes Yawgoog's 10th Reservation Director

- 1995 Medicine Bow waterfront cabin gets a major refurbishment; A. Richard Greene becomes Yawgoog's 11th Reservation Director; Medicine Bow dining hall gets a new roof; 13th National Scout Jamboree attended by RI Scouts at Fort A. P. Hill, VA; Al Gunther retired after 36 years as second Camp Ranger, Fire Chief and EMT
- 1996 Three Point waterfront cabin gets a major refurbishment. Sandy Beach staff office gets expanded to double its size; Paul Forbes became 3rd Yawgoog Ranger; the Medicine Bow waterfront was redesigned and rebuilt, and dedicated to Ranger Al Gunther
- 1997 Sandy Beach waterfront gets rebuilt, but keeping intact the 2-story original design—a bigger, more spacious building is up!; A former staffman creates the first website dedicated to Yawgoog; 14th National Scout Jamboree attended by RI Scouts at Fort A. P. Hill, VA
- 1999 International Scout exchange program started with Dominican Republic, Emmanuel Gonzalez and Larissa Paniagua hired on Medicine Bow staff

2000-Present

- 2000 Thomas Sisson named first year-round, full-time Yawgoog Reservation Director; two Dominicans staff hired: Giselle Gonzolez in MB and George Castillo in Sandy Beach
- 2001 Dominican Scouts staff were George Castillo returning to the Beach and Iv'n Filpo in Three Point; 15th National Scout Jamboree attended by RI Scouts at Fort A. P. Hill, VA
- 2002 Three Dominican staff were Jonathan de Camps at the Beach, Jose Luis de Cruz at 3-Point, and Dario de Los Santos at the Bow. Challenge Valley, a mud course across from Ashaway opens. Geocaching introduced at Camp Craft with an accompanying GPS segment.
- 2003 88th Yawgoog season June 29 through August 24, 2003; Medicine Bow kitchen rebuilt; four Dominican staff are Ronny Ventura at 3-Point, Rosmery Rojas and Dario de Los Santos at the Bow, and Jonathan Rojas at the Beach; Paul Forbes recognized for 25 years of Ranger service to Camp Yawgoog; Yawgoog Heritage Center dedicated August 2, 2003 at the Yawgoog Alumni Association reunion; front porch of main Trading Post dedicated to Joe Herbold for his long service to camp on staff and as 2nd Chairman of the Yawgoog Alumni Association (YAA) from 1986 to 2003; Stephen F. Dolan named 3rd YAA chairman.
- 2004 Porch Built onto Medicine Bow Dining Hall with three new sets of stairs, fire alarm systems fully operational at each dining hall
- 2005 Norovirus hits Yawgoog at the end of week four, forcing the closure for week five and six. 16 National Scout Jamboree attended by Rhode Island Scouts at Fort A.P. Hill, VA

- 2006 Yawgoog starts converting open pit latrines into flush toilets, beginning with Medicine Bow The "Barn" opens teaching Farm Mechanics and Plumbing.
- 2007 Open pit latrines in Three Point are converted into flush toilets.
- 2008 Flush Toilets are on for all Campsites.
- 2009 Phase III of the Yawgoog ISDS project was completed.
- 2010 Boy Scouts of America and the Rhode Island Boy Scouts are celebrating their 100th Anniversary.

The Sisson Shelter was built in 1998 to honor Eagle Scout John Sisson from Troop 138 West Kingston. John was killed shortly after his 18th birthday by a drunk driver while helping some friends change a flat tire. John loved Aquapaug and spent many summers there working with the Cub Scout Day Camp as a Den Leader. It is fitting that this memorial be in his honor in a place he loved so much.

HISTORY OF THE MEMORIAL BELL TOWER AT YAWGOOG

Written by H. Cushman "Gus" Anthony

On August 8, 1943, the original Memorial Bell Tower was dedicated in honor of those Scouts and Scouters who had died for God and Country during World War II. The inscription then as now reads, "WHEN YOU HEAR THIS BELL, REMEMBER SCOUTS WHO DIED FOR GOD AND COUNTRY." In that year, we probably all knew at least one of the 319 Scouts who had been killed and many came from homes where a Gold Star Flag was displayed in the front window.

The 300-pound bell was a gift to the Camp from Troop 1 Wakefield. It was originally a bell from a mill. 'Chief' Williams conceived the memorial idea and asked "Inky" Armstrong, our Camp Ranger at that time, to create such a tower. "Inky" contacted Doug Gardiner, a Seabee stationed in Alaska and a former member of "Slade's Gang," who had also helped with the plans of the Metcalf Lodge. Doug carried out the Bucklin Memorial's heavy timber idea. Probably George Parkhurst, our camp carpenter on Inky's crew, did most of the actual construction.

The daily ringing of the bell 12 times every noon almost immediately gave birth to another wonderful Yawgoog tradition. Spontaneously and without any direction, Scouts and leaders all over the reservation would stop whatever they were doing, stand up with head bowed and hat in hand remembering those former Yawgoog Campers who had died for God and Country.

Another tradition for many years was a Memorial Day Service at the J. Harold Williams Amphitheatre, which included the tolling of the bell. This service was jointly attended by the Scouts and leaders that were in camp that weekend, plus a group of some 25 or 30 young men and women who were taking their Water Safety Training at Three Point under the able leadership of Harold Anderson of the American Red Cross. Yawgoog is proud of all its traditions!

Two other uses of this Memorial Bell should be recorded. It is tolled every Sunday morning to call the Scouts of their respective Worship Services in our three religious centers. Also, in case of a fire or a water accident, it is rung to round up those specially trained staff members.

So, today as the bell tolls, let us all 'remember Scouts who died for God and Country' in all of our wars and encounters of all years. May this great Yawgoog tradition be carried on through countless generations of Yawgoog campers. God bless them all and may peace be with us forever.

Last . . . but certainly not least is a brief bio of one of the most beloved icons of Scouting in the Narragansett Council . . . H. Cushman "Gus" Anthony . . . the name synonymous with Scouting in Rhode Island.

H. CUSHMAN 'GUS' ANTHONY

March 7, 1904 to August 2, 2000

Born on March 7, 1904, Gus Anthony was the son of William Gardner Anthony and Ruth Gilman Cushman Anthony. The family lived in a stately house on Euclid Avenue, on the East Side. Gus was educated in the Providence Public School system graduating in 1922 from Hope High School. In March 1915, as a student at the Slater Avenue School, Gus joined the Boy Scouts 3rd Providence Troop. His Scoutmaster was a 17-year old named J. Harold Williams, who would go on to lead the Narragansett Council Boy Scouts of America from 1918 until 1962.

Chief Williams was the greatest influence on Mr. Anthony, who worked closely with him for decades. Gus was among the first Boy Scouts to attend Camp Yawgoog in Hopkinton, which opened in 1916. He returned for 52 summers, first as a camper, then, starting in 1921, as part of the staff. He was Camp Director from 1951 to 1968. In the Council's collection of photos is included a picture of Gus driving U.S. Senator Claiborne Pell and his wife, Nuala, around the camp in his trademark 1921 Model T which he called the 'Funeral Coach'.

Even after his retirement, Gus was a frequent visitor to the camp, always in his uniform. In 1981, he established the Yawgoog Alumni Association, which now has about 1,300 members nationwide. He co-wrote "The Yawgoog Story" with Williams in 1985 and in 1990, he helped to organize Yawgoog's 75th Anniversary Party, which drew about 800 people. "My greatest love in Scouting was camping", said Anthony in 1993. Gus joined the Council's Professional Staff as a Field Executive in 1927, after five years at Brown University, where he was part of the Class of 1926 and had completed one year of graduate work in biology. He met his wife, the late Martha Jane (Kiser) Anthony, of Kentucky, through his work. She was a psychiatric social worker and wanted to enroll one of her charges in Camp Yawgoog. They talked in his office and then he asked if they could continue the discussion over dinner. They were married in October 1933 and they had one daughter, Gwendolyn Anthony Mazanetz, and two grandchildren; Thomas Anthony Mazanetz, who is an Eagle Scout, and Martha L. Donnell.

As the Narragansett Council grew, Gus rose through the ranks. In 1939 he became Assistant Scout Executive and Chief of Staff under Williams. In September 1962, he became Deputy Scout Executive. Mr. Anthony retired on March 1, 1969, but continued to serve on the Finance and Advisory Committees of the Narragansett Council. Gwendolyn once said, "Dad fell in love with Scouting as a young kid and he really tried to follow the Scout principles. You were to serve God and you were to serve your country, and you were loyal, and you were friendly . . . this is how Gus lived his life." Even as he lay dying in a hospice bed, he bid farewell to his grandson with a Scout salute.

Scouting wasn't the only love in Gus' life. He had a true love for people and the ability to help when he could. He also served on the Board of Directors of the New England Section of the American Camping Association. He was class president, reunion chairman and class fund agent for the Brown Class of 1926, and he walked down College hill every year at graduation until 1999. Gus was active with the Providence Art Club, served on the buildings and grounds committee of the Rhode Island Historical Society and was on the advisory committee of the Providence Preservation Society. He was head usher and deacon at the Central Congregational Church for more than three-quarters of a century and he was founder and co-chairman of the Concerned Citizens of the East Side, which sought to quiet down Thayer Street. Gus was also active in senior citizens' affairs. He served on the Governor's Council on Aging and on the Commission on Care and Safety of the Elderly, and he was on the Board of Directors of Hamilton House and of Home Health Services of Rhode Island.

H. Cushman "Gus" Anthony . . . here at the 1996 Yawgoog Alumni Reunion. Gus is center stage holding the sign. Sitting to Gus's left is his old friend W. Chesley 'Chet' Worthington—both graduates of Brown University.

Gus did not go unrecognized for his many great works. He received his first medal way back in March of 1917 from the RI Animal Rescue League for rescuing a very fat cat from a 'big' dog (wish I knew more about this story!). In 1959 Brown University awarded Gus with a Citation for 'discharging the offices of life with usefulness and reputation'. In 1968 he received the top New England Award from the American Camping Association and in 1969 the Narragansett Council awarded him the Bucklin Medal with three stars. In 1975 The Providence Art Club presented Gus with an original, autographed copy of George Minor's book entitled, "Angell's Lane" for deep concern and devotion to the Club and his faithfulness over the years. Also in 1975 Gus was awarded the highest award given to a Scouting volunteer, the Silver Beaver Award. In 1979 the American Red Cross gave Gus the 'Distinguished Service Award'.

The "H. Cushman Anthony Craft Center" was dedicated to Gus by the Yawgoog Alumni Association in 1981 and in 1982 the Roman Catholic Diocese of Rhode Island awarded him with the St. George Medal 'in recognition of outstanding service to the spiritual development of Catholic Youth in the program of the Boy Scouts of America'. In 1985, Gus was inducted into the Rhode Island Heritage Hall of Fame and the following year, he was one of 350 Providence residents to receive Special Citizen Awards for the city's 350th Anniversary. Then in 1991, the Brown Alumni Association awarded Gus 'The Brown Bear Award' for outstanding personal service rendered the University over a period of time. On September 15th, 1995, he also received from Brown University the "H. Anthony Ittleson '60 Award" for his Annual Fund Raising which culminated in 100% of his class donating. In November of 1995, Gus received the "Robert W. McCreanor Award" from the Department of Elderly Affairs for 'Outstanding contributions to the Older Citizens of RI'. This award was given to him by Governor Almond. In addition, Gus received four Rhode Island State Legislative Citations over the years.

'Smiling' Gus Anthony at the 1995 Narragansett Council Annual Recognition Dinner.
Then Program Director, Mike Donaghue, is standing behind Gus.

All unit leaders were invited to submit history and photos of their unit. The following Unit Histories were submitted voluntarily and all entries received were included as part of the *'The First 100 Years of Scouting in the Narragansett Council 1910 to 2010".*

Unit Histories

Troop 1 Gaspee Kitchen at Rhodes

TROOP 1 GASPEE PLATEAU

- Date of Original Charter: **9/30/1932**

- Notable Alumni
  - John Bennett—John was the troop's first Eagle in 1937. It is believed that he was the first Eagle in the City of Warwick.
  - Donald Knee—West Shore District's Scouter of the Year in 1968.
  - Robert "Jay" Pease—Former President of Narragansett Council.
  - Robert "Bob" Barnes—Served as Council Commissioner twice.
  - Bruce Ingham—Long time member of Yawgoog Alumni Association. Vice Chair of YAA from 1986 to 2004. Long time Yawgoog staff member, including camp director. Former scoutmaster of Troop 1.
  - Charles DeBevoise—Long time member of Yawgoog Alumni Association. Secretary of YAA from 1986 to 2003. Long time Yawgoog staff member.
  - Stephen Dolan—Long time member of Yawgoog Alumni Association. Current Treasurer of YAA. Served as YAA Chair from 2003-2009 and Treasurer from 1988 to 2003. Long time Yawgoog staff member.
  - Nicholas Smalley—Nick is the most decorated Gaspee scout in recent memory, if not in troop history. Nick is an Eagle with 7 palms, and has earned 72 merit badges. He served the troop in a variety of junior leadership roles, and continues as an ASM. Nick is a Vigil member of the Order of the Arrow, and served as the Abnaki Lodge elections chair as a youth. Nick

also served as the SPL to one of the Narragansett Council's 2005 National Jamboree troops.

Troop 1 Gaspee Plateau has been camping at Yawgoog for as long as anyone can remember. It has been staying at Dan Boone during Week 3 since at least the 1950's. A troop portrait from 1948 lists the campsite as Lewis and Clark. During the late 70's and early 80's the troop stayed both week 1 at Paul Siple and week 3 at Dan Boone.

Troop 1 Gaspee Yawgoog or Bust

A Brief History of Troop 1 Gaspee Plateau from 1932 to 2009

Troop 1 Gaspee Plateau was chartered in Warwick, Rhode Island on September 30, 1932 by a "Group of Citizens" under the leadership of Scoutmaster Norman Edwards and Committee Chair Fred Bolduc. The troop has been based out of Asbury United Methodist Church for most if not all of its history. It was sponsored by various civic groups from Asbury and the Gaspee area, until the church itself took over as sponsor in the early 1980's. It has been meeting at 7:00 PM on Wednesday nights at Asbury for as long as anyone can remember.

The troop dubbed in its first Eagle, John Bennett, on August 26, 1937. It was recently reported to the troop that John was the first Eagle Scout in Warwick, although this has not been confirmed. John's father was a key contributor in the early days of Narragansett Council and the West Shore district.

The troop continued through most of the 30's, 40's, and early 50's under the direction of William McKenna, Cyril Pratt, and Donald Cady. They left behind a rich archive of charters, photographs, and other documentation that has helped preserve the troop's history. In July 1942, the troop participated in the "Yawgoog or Bust" canoe expedition, traveling by canoe from the Edgewood Yacht Club down Narragansett Bay, through rivers and ponds to Yawgoog. During WWII, the troop was affiliated with Sea Scout Ship Commodore Francis B Stone. The troop's trademark totem poles and sign were carved by the troop in the mid 1940's. They were the centerpiece of the troop's Indian

Lore display at the 1947 pow-wow camporee. These cherished relics continue to serve as the troop's gateway every year at summer camp.

The troop continued to be very active in the 1950's under the direction of Art Schweikart and Red Salisbury. In 1957, Bill Aldrich, Russ McKenna, John Sheppard, and Bill Pettis joined the Narragansett Council's delegation to the Fourth National Jamboree at Valley Forge, PA. The troop continued to be active at Yawgoog and in the West Shore district in the 1960's, with Charlie Jones taking over as Scoutmaster. In the late 1960's, the troop obtained its troop trailer, a 1944 US Army jeep trailer. It continues to serve the troop 40 years later.

The 1970's were a great time for Troop 1 Gaspee Plateau. The troop flourished under the direction of scoutmasters Charlie Jones, Bruce Ingham, and Donald Brunt. Featuring a high adventure program and lots of camping, the troop grew to over 40 scouts by the end of the decade. The annual camping schedule developed in the 70's remains largely intact in 2009, featuring the mountain climbing trip, commando overnighter, winter cabins, bike hike, and canoe trip. The distinctive "Hubba Hubba Ding Ding" troop cheer was started in the early 70's, and continues to roar across Medicine Bow dining hall every summer. Also around this time, the troop began its practice of having troop neckerchiefs, T-shirts, and hats made, mostly bearing the HMS Gaspee silhouette logo. Unlike most troops, Gaspee changes its t-shirt and hat colors almost every year, and has issued over 30 different shirts and hats over the years. Many of the troop's Eagles and alumni of this era stayed active in scouting, both with the troop and at Yawgoog. Gaspee was everywhere, and in 1974 10% of the Yawgoog staff was from Troop 1. To this day, the Gaspee alumni from the 1970's continue to contribute to Yawgoog, serving in key roles on the executive board of the Yawgoog Alumni Association.

The troop continued to prosper in the early 1980's under Scoutmaster Donald Brunt. The troop continued to be a dominant force at Yawgoog, and had a spirited rivalry with Troop 3 Seekonk. Jim Melvin became the troop's 50th Eagle during the troop's 50th anniversary year of 1982. In the years after Mr. Brunt left, the troop stumbled a bit. Chuck DeBevoise, Eagle Scout and SPL from the mid-70's, stepped in and helped get the program back on track. Marty Hebert briefly served as scoutmaster, and helped stabilize the troop. Tim Lavine then took over for the remainder of the decade. Troop 1 Cranston joined us in Dan Boone at Yawgoog for a number of years. The two troops formed a strong bond, until 1 Cranston lost membership and disbanded. Gaspee and Cranston buried a time capsule in Dan Boone one of their summers together. We talk about digging it up every year, but have yet to do it. During the mid 80's, the totem poles and trailer underwent extensive restorations by the troop's junior leaders. The troop then faltered again in the late 80's, and membership dropped dangerously low.

Troop 1 Gaspee 1986 Mt. Lafayette Summit

Gaspee Eagles John and Jim Gosselin took over as Scoutmaster and Committee Chair in 1990 and gradually rebuilt the troop. Within a few years, membership was back up and the program was rolling again. The troop began its tradition of 100% attendance at Yawgoog daily worship services, which continues to this day. The troop began to welcome female adult leaders in the 90's, at a time when this was not always popular. In 1996, John moved to Committee Chair and Gaspee Eagle Gerry Terceiro took over as Scoutmaster. They continue in these roles to present day. Strong recruiting classes in 1998 and 1999 would carry the troop into the next century, eventually producing 8 Eagles. In 1999, a reunion of 1970's alumni was held, drawing many of them back into closer contact with the troop.

As the 21st century dawned, Troop 1 Gaspee Plateau continued to grow and prosper. The troop has dubbed 18 Eagles this decade, the most of any decade in its history, and it is not even over yet. These boys provided strong youth leadership, and moved the troop back to a more boy led program. In 2005, under the direction of SPL Nick Smalley and ASPL Jeff Berthelette, the troop won the honor of Week 3 Troop of the Week at Medicine Bow. It was the first time the troop had won since the early 80's. In the late 00's, a second troop trailer was purchased to augment our WWII classic. At Yawgoog, Troop 1 formed a bond with Troops 138 West Kingston and 44 Glocester, with the 3 units adopting the URI Fight Song as their joint cheer. In recent years, more ambitious trips have been added to the schedule, including Washington DC in 2007 and Gettysburg in 2009.

In 2007, the troop celebrated its 75th anniversary with a reunion and family night. The troop now has strong adult leadership, with involvement of both parents and alumni. Many Eagles continue on with the troop as adult leaders. Gerry Terceiro, John Gosselin, and Jim Gosselin continue to lead the troop, with important contributions this decade from adult leaders Jason Richards, John Kelsall, Al Blais, Jon VanLoon, Mike Hedley, and many others. In recent years, the troop has forged a stronger bond with Pack 1 Gaspee Plateau, helping them build a stronger Cub Scout outdoor program. The next generation is coming, with the sons and nephews of the troop leadership moving up through the pack. It is hoped that the support and strengthening of its feeder pack will help propel Troop 1 into the next decade.

Throughout its 77 years, Troop 1 Gaspee Plateau has survived many ups and downs. Key to its endurance has been its outdoor program, respect for tradition, and close knit family atmosphere. From the totem poles, to the WWII trailer, to the troop cheer, to its camping traditions, to the ancient black and white photos in its archives, the symbols of its past continue to play key roles in its present. The troop's 82 Eagles are a testament to its commitment to developing character and leadership in the young men of Warwick. The oral history is passed through the years, and its Eagles keep coming back to inspire and lead the next generation. Its core leadership is entering its 4th decade with the troop and is showing no sign of slowing down. With an adventurous program, a great bunch of boys, supportive adults, and a strong feeder pack, Troop 1 Gaspee Plateau looks forward to being around for its 100th anniversary in 2032.

Eagle Scouts from Troop 1 Gaspee Plateau:

William P. Aldrich	**08/04/56**
Steven L. Bailey	**0/02/95**
John N. Bennett	**08/26/37**
Jeffrey Louis Berthelette	**08/16/06**
Kurt Jay Bittner	**10/27/76**
Corey Andre Blais	05/06/00
Kevin Thomas Brooks	**08/07/97**
Donald P. Brown	**12/17/62**
Donald R. Brunt	**08/18/80**

Donald R. Bryant	01/01/80
John Andrew Candido	06/30/97
Vincent D. Capuano	11/14/77
Michael L. Chartier	08/12/08
Allen T. Chase	10/28/01
John Marshall Cohen	08/15/54
Matthew T. Collins	01/22/90
John M. Coogan	06/13/80
Frederick I. Crossman, Jr.	12/19/95
Charles H. DeBevoise	09/01/72
Stephen F. Dolan	04/12/76
Frederick S. Ey	02/26/68
Robert S. Follett	06/17/68
William Garcia	02/27/95
John H. Gosselin	09/05/85
Jim T. Gossellin	09/04/85
Terrence D. Gray	04/17/79
Howard Haronian	11/14/77
Derek Michael Hatzberger	08/16/06
Matthew Michael Hedley	03/08/06
Frank J. Hoelldorfer	08/24/44
James M. Jaques III	12/14/57
Gregory C. Kelsall	10/13/05
Jason Allen Kelsall	10/28/01
Donald K. Knee, Jr.	08/13/61
Kevin G. Lambert	05/19/88
Harry Lefebvre, Jr.	04/03/48
Jesse James Lewis	05/08/03
Robert F. MacDonald	12/17/62
Edward J. McEntee	07/30/59
Everett E. McEwen, Jr.	04/03/48
Russell E. McKenna, Jr.	12/17/55
James A. Melvin	09/13/82
Jason Edward Metivier	06/24/04
Andrew Chandler Morgan	04/15/04
Cole Alexander Morgan	12/17/08
William Moskosky	02/21/66
Stephen Norris	11/20/61

Stephen O'Neill	01/23/73
Bruce Pease	05/08/64
Robert H. Pease, Jr.	11/20/63
Robert Alexis Pelletier-Carlos	12/17/08
Robert L. Pratt	12/27/43
Andrew Leslie Quackenbush	09/30/09
David P. Randall	09/13/82
Michael P. Reinke	04/09/86
Timothy E. Reinke	08/26/80
Jason S. Richards	09/01/93
Michael D. Richards	09/05/91
John Robert Rowan, Jr.	01/01/98
Paul Safferson	11/28/77
Daniel Santos	10/11/73
James A. Schweikart	03/11/63
Walter A. Schweikart	12/13/58
Nicholas D. Smalley	04/08/04
Robert W. Sprague	11/14/77
Andrew K. Stone	08/18/80
Gerard Sullivan	09/10/73
William H. Tatro	11/20/63
Gerald E. Terceiro	04/14/86
Chris J. VanLoon	01/19/05
John A. Wallace	04/03/48
Howard White	05/17/65
Peter Wyman	09/10/73

TROOP 1 KINGSTON

Troop 1 began meeting at the Kingston Congregational Church, where its founding Scoutmaster was the Church's minister. Meetings have been held at various locations including the Rhode Island State College (now URI), the Tavern Hall Club, Scoutland, and mostly in the Church.

In 1927, a local farmer, Arthur N. Peckham deeded to the Tavern Hall Club 6+ acres of woodland off Old North Road for use only by "the Scout troop that meets in Kingston" as a campsite. Originally the troop called the site "Peckham Camp" with its "Scout House" building. Later a fire destroyed the building but its stone chimney remains. Now the site is called "Scoutland." In 2004 Scoutland title was transferred to the South Kingstown Land Trust to be preserved for the exclusive use of Kingston's Boy Scouts.

The troop has a long history of summer camping at Yawgoog's Three Point, with the exception of a period in the 1970s, returning in the summer of 1981, and continuously since. Many years the troop was recognized as the Point's outstanding troop of week #7. The troop did go through some difficult times early in World War II, the mid-1960s, and late-1970s when membership and advancement declined. But each time with new leadership Troop 1 came through stronger to be recognized as one of the outstanding troops in southern Rhode Island.

In 1996 with the troop having over 80 registered Scouts, divided spinning-off the new Troop 138 West Kingston with Tom Sisson as Scoutmaster. Scouts and leaders have camped at West Point, Florida Sea Base, Philmont, Block Island, Aquapaug, Quonset, National Jamborees, Council & District Jamborees, with many mountain hikes, white water rafting, and other adventures. In the early 1960s a patrol of older Scouts took a two-month cross-country road trip in an old VW bus camping along the way. Scouts have gone on high adventure international trips to the Dominican Republic in 2000, '04, '06, '08 and '10 with plans to return in 2012 led by a past Scoutmaster.

Many former Troop 1 Scouts have served with distinction in the US military, universities, business, and government, with many returning as adult Scout leaders in Kingston and elsewhere. The troop has proudly operated continuously without break for wars or depression, giving significant service to the youth of Kingston, RI, area for 87 years.

Many former Troop 1 Scouts have served with distinction in the US military, universities, business, and government, with many returning at adult Scout leaders in Kingston and elsewhere. The troop has proudly operated continuously without break for wars or depression, giving significant service to the youth of Kingston, RI, area for 87 years.

SCOUTMASTERS & YEARS OF SERVICE—TROOP 1 KINGSTON

1923 Rev. Egbert W. A. Jenkinson
1924 Harry L. Thomas
1925-28 Rev. Claude G. Beardslee
1929 George R. Champlin
1930-32 Jesse Prime
1933-34 Robert H. DeWolf
1935-38 George A. Thompson, Jr.

1961 Erwin Johnson
1962 Frank Dieraul, Jr.
1963-64 David Meekings
1965-67 Kimball Green
1967-69 & 73 Philip Very
1970 Richard Kenney
1971-72 Joseph Vanryzin

1939 E. Howard Nichols
1940 ?
1941 Ralph C. Lewis
1942-43 Russell E. Larson
1944-46 Robert S. Bell
1947-49 Bruce Britton
1950-51 Roger H. Bender
1952-53 Warren Hagist
1954 Robert Harrison
1955 Frederick Warren
1955-56 Earl R. Bond
1957 Fred Kenney
1958-60 Bancroft Henderson, Jr.

1974-76 Philip Nelson
1976 William Carberry
1977-79 A. David McNab
1980-81 Bruce C. Dunham
1981 Nate Barrington
1981-82 & 84-85 Neil W. Ross
1983 & 1986 James T. McWeeney
1987-88 Stephen D. Anderson
1989-96 James F. Mulhearn
1996-98 Edward H. Dettmann
1999-02 Peter Nunes
2002-05 Neil Murray
2005-08 Darryl Keith
2008-Present, James Given

EAGLE STATISTICS

- Troop 1 Kingston's first 59 years produced 18 Eagle Scouts. In the past 28 years awards were given to 59 Eagles or 78%, with 18 (23%) earned in the 1990's and 30 (39%) in the first decade of the 21st Century. More are on the way.
- 14 sets of brothers made Eagle in Kingston, with 2 families of 3 Eagles each.
- 17 Eagles are sons of Eagles and one has an Eagle grandfather.

77 EAGLE SCOUTS, as of August 2010

1. Millard Fillmore Perry, Jr. 1931
2. Carroll D. Billmyer, Jr. 1934
3. John Peleg Barlow 1936
4. Lester Hartwell Bills 1936
5. Robert Aukerman 1958
6. Bruce E. Walker 1959
7. Basil Edson DeWolf 1961
8. William Clinton Metz 1961
9. David Ernest Meekings 1962
10. John C. Lewis 1962
11. James Vance Aukerman 1962
12. Keith Howard Munroe 1962
13. Jack K. Guy 1963
14. Kevin Scott Munroe 1964

40. John William Tarasevich 1997
41. Pasquale Stephen DeMatteo 1998
42. Joseph Paul Daley 1999
43. Philip Brandi Johnson 1999
44. Peter Joseph Johnson 1999
45. Robert Jess Dettmann 2000
46. Wyatt Charles Messinger 2000
47. Christopher Michael Ridings 2000
48. Ryan Patrick Murphy 2001
49. David Michael Mangiante 2002
50. Jack Layton Bergersen 2003
51. David Edward Petrucci 2004
52. Matthew Scott Alemany 2004
53. Patrick Day Marran 2004

15. Kenneth Dawson Wood 1964
16. Richard Alan Kenney 1965
17. Philip Miles Wood 1975
18. Stephen Lathrop Wood 1978
19. Jonathan Wayne Naughton 1982
20. Edward Robert Lawson, Jr. 1984
21. David Myron Cohen 1987
22. Jonathan David Goldstein 1987
23. Lincoln Neil Ross 1987
24. David Mathew Jakubowski 1987
25. Jeffrey Todd McWeeney 1988
26. Brook Williams Ross 1989
27. Ram Anand Narasimhan 1990
28. James Robert Liguori 1991
29. Sam Paul Lemay 1991
30. Christopher Thomas McHugh 1991
31. Seth Helsel Crothers 1992
32. William John Palm IV 1992
33. Adam John Durant 1992
34. Scott Keegan Munroe 1992
35. Edward W. Svehlik 1993
36. David Benjamin Coleman 1994
37. Michael James Mulhearn 1994
38. Dana Clark Seaton 1996
39. Andrew Simpson Palm 1997

54. Brandon Joel Keith 2005
55. Daniel John Desaulniers 2005
56. Jeffrey David Coons Jr. 2005
57. Michael John Mangiante 2005
58. Peter Michael Tarasevich 2006
59. Mark Joseph Alemany 2006
60. Timothy Corbett Marran 2006
61. Robert Ryan DelPrete 2006
62. Denis Patrick Murray 2007
63. Evan Daniel Barksdale Keith 2007
64. Zachary Aleksander Kotlow 2007
65. Raymond Henry Barry 2007
66. Patrick William Morrison 2007
67. Kenneth John Burke Jr. 2007
68. David Michael Alemany 2007
69. James Patrick Given Jr. 2007
70. Frank Swinney LiVolsi 2008
71. Brandon Michael Kotlow 2008
72. Anthony Dennis Pincince 2009
73. Michael Brecht Morrison 2009
74. Sean Michael Marran 2009
75. Anthony James Ricciutti 2010
76. Alexander Brian Briggs 2010
77. Zachary Grant Briggs 2010

TROOP 1 NORTH SCITUATE

Troop 1 North Scituate was organized in January 1926 under the leadership of Theodore H. Hopkins. 14 Scouts were listed on the first charter along with three committee members. Meetings were held on Tuesday evenings at the North Scituate Grammar School. In 1932, the location of meetings changed to the Town Council Chambers.

Due to age restrictions, the troop designated William Straw as a token Scoutmaster in 1933. Oscar Grissom assumed leadership of the troop, which spent the entire year building a cabin from the wood of a house targeted for demolition. The cabin, complete with a front porch, was erected on state property across from the Trinity Episcopal Church. The troop named the site "Camp Oscawawa" and conducted meetings there during the summer. William Straw's property was adjacent to the site and the figurehead would occasionally pay the troop a visit until the state denied permission for the troop to use the land.

In 1934, the troop participated in the annual Scouting Jamboree held on North Main Street in Providence, where troops were allowed only 15 minutes to complete their exhibitions. Troop 1 constructed a tower made entirely of timber and rope. There were 13 sections tied with ropes using every lashing recommended by the Boy Scout Manual. The tower was sturdy enough to climb and supported the weight of the scouts. The troop had previously built a duplicate tower at "Camp Oscawawa" and successfully transmitted radio signals between the two towers.

The American Legion, Post 19, became the sponsor for Troop 1 in 1937. Ralph Shuman was a member of the Legion and Scoutmaster that same year. He left the troop to be district commissioner of the Woonasquatucket District. He was awarded the Silver Beaver Award for his work over the years of World War II.

Scoutmaster Lester Fales recalls generating enough money from newspaper drives to send each scout to Camp Yawgoog for a week and also pay for a year's subscription to Boy's Life magazine. Another memorable activity was collecting aluminum pots and pans to assist in the war effort. The Providence Journal published a picture of the huge pile of aluminum, which was where the fire station is currently located. In 1941, the troop developed a scout campsite behind the Moswansicut Rod and Gun Club. It was called "Camp Douglas Burnside" in memory of a former scout who died in his early manhood. His father, Maurice Burnside, erected a steel flagpole in his memory and presented the troop with a large American flag to be flown. A bridge was built across the brook as well.

In 1951, the troop obtained new facilities in the basement of the Community House. Scout Hall continues to be the meeting place of the troop. Troop 1 has owned three school busses, one of which was towed from Bellows Falls, Vermont to North Scituate in 1978. A "bus fund" had been established to pay for repairs.

Some highlights have been trips to Mt. Washington, the Battleship Massachusetts, Valley Forge, Fort Ticonderoga, the Boston Museum of Science, New York City, LaSalette Shrine, the Newport Naval Base, Tunbridge Fair in Vermont, the Christmas Lights in Connecticut and even to the island of Bermuda.

The troop continues to host the annual Beanhole Bake every February, hold meetings on Thursday evening, go swimming once a month at the Wanskuk Boys and Girls Club and invade campsite Kit Carson at Sandy Beach every summer at Camp Yawgoog during Week 1. It also participates in service projects, tree plantings, a cookie sale during the annual Scituate Art Festival. Troop 1 North Scituate was also part of the honor guard at Senator John Chafee's funeral in 1999.

Troop 1 North Scituate Eagle Scouts:

James R. Adams	06/22/68
John D. Adams	06/22/68
John Allan	12/15/56
Douglas Allan, Jr.	12/15/56
Darrell B. Anger	08/02/07
Raymond R. Antonelli	04/25/80
James M. Archetto	11/14/77
Paul V. Archetto	06/18/86
Charles J. Barden	04/11/77
Gilbert Barden	12/15/73
Jeffrey A. Bartlett	06/01/83
Jason P. Bonin	08/02/97
Bruce Coe Bowker	06/22/68
Paul Leonard Carlson	10/30/95
Peter Charles Carlson	10/30/95
Darek T. Chadwick	10/16/89
Corey Daniel Charest	01/01/99
Gregory J. Charest	09/24/02
Patrick James Charest	11/15/05
Derek Robert Coia	11/05/09
James A. Coia	06/15/06
Charles Allen Collins, III	10/07/97
Arthur Cook	12/05/38
Charles B. Cost	05/17/94
Daniel H. Cost	06/24/92
Michael N. Cost	11/23/94
Thaddeus A. Czernick	03/07/79
David Macdonald D'Agostino	01/20/89
Daniel E. DeYear	12/14/74
Donald J. Dennehy	09/10/83
Charles H. Diggle	01/13/76
Gary Diggle	08/28/72
Geoffrey Diggle	01/23/74
James A. Diggle	04/11/77
Kenneth A. Diggle	02/05/80
Howard A. Diggle, Jr.	06/02/83
John Philip Dorr	02/26/09
Martin S. Doyle	01/23/74

David E. Duhaime	09/22/66
Dennis A. Duhaime	04/10/67
Roland J. Duhaime	02/11/85
Gilbert E. Duhaime, Jr.	12/05/80
Louis W. Dunn	12/06/37
Lester P. Fales, Jr.	12/06/37
Steve P. Finn	06/27/86
John E. Geisser	12/30/83
John Goding	08/28/72
Eric E. Gould	04/10/67
William Gould	09/26/77
Brian K. Gowdy	03/29/84
Herbert A. Gowdy, Jr.	11/07/80
John Greenwood	08/26/43
Havis Grissom	04/05/37
John H. Grissom	03/25/85
Maurice B. Grissom	12/06/37
Oscar Grissom, Jr.	12/06/37
Allen C. Huestis	08/13/61
Howard Paul Jehan	06/22/68
Walter E. Joslin	11/14/78
Paul R. Lamore	01/23/74
Edward Albert Lanoue	02/06/89
Geoffrey Richard Lemieux	01/01/99
Mark Lemieux	01/15/02
Bernard Lemire	08/18/49
Joseph Michael Lenihan	12/13/58
Jeffrey M. Liptrop	12/05/80
Robert N. Liptrot	04/11/77
Stephen P. Maguire	02/05/80
Scott Maker	08/30/72
Craig M. McCannon	12/05/80
Craig McGannon	01/01/81
Roger Medbury	04/08/57
Erik W. Mikkelsen	10/22/87
Scott N. Miller	11/14/77
David G. Mink	05/22/79
Wayne A. Monroe	03/07/79
Donald Parker Morrison, Jr.	01/23/74
Stephen Bernard Nelson	01/25/07

Ralph E. Olney, III	01/15/68
Joseph John Paliotti	03/24/05
Robert Payton	01/23/74
Glenn G. Perry	06/22/68
Eric P. Petsching	09/26/77
Kevin M. Piatek	07/11/88
David J. Picard	10/11/77
Michael E. Picard	10/11/77
Steven R. Pittman	05/07/82
Robert Poyton	01/23/74
Stephen Raymond Pratt, Jr.	10/23/95
Peter Previte	10/07/08
Steven M. Proulx	10/26/84
Scott R. Rivard	05/04/91
Jon Henry Roy	03/24/05
Stanley Russell	08/04/56
Thomas Russell	08/04/56
Stephen J. Sargent	11/13/84
Bradford C. Sherman	01/02/71
Edgar L. Shuman	12/06/37
Alan Sparn	01/23/74
Daniel G. Stephens	01/01/80
David G. Stephens	01/18/80
John N. Stephens	06/22/83
Nicholas Scott Stephens	08/14/08
Glenn Thompson	02/05/80
Mark D. Thompson	01/23/74
Donald B. Tipple, Jr.	04/08/57
Mark Ullucci	09/16/96
Paul A. Ullucci	10/26/84
John F. Valentine IV	10/23/95
Stephen Andrew Vigliotti	01/01/99
Kent Watson	01/23/74
Kirk E. Watson	05/07/82
Dana B. Westberg	01/15/68
Robert W. Wigsten	03/07/79
Patrick Joseph Willis	10/07/97
John F. Winfield, Jr.	08/29/78
William L. Young	11/07/80

FIRST PROVIDENCE TROOP

The First Providence Troop was organized during 1910 under the leadership of Herbert R. Dean. A total of 64 Scouts were listed on the First Charter. Troop meetings were held at the Broad Street School in the Washington Park section of Providence. On October 24, 1910, the First Providence Troop was officially recognized at Boy Scout headquarters in Providence. Dr. Raymond F. Hacking was called "the first Boy Scout" because he was the "First Sergeant" (Senior Patrol Leader of the First Providence Troop.

On May 23, 1911, the First Providence Troop joined with other troops for the first public appearance of the Rhode Island Boy Scouts. The occasion was the presentation of the troop flags to be presented at the State House by Mrs. A.J. Pothier, wife of the Governor of Rhode Island. The First Providence Troop stood proudly in front of the assembled troops and Scoutmaster Dean was the first to advance up the stairs and receive the first troop flag from Mrs. Pothier.

On May 28, 1911, the First Providence Troop, along with 13 other troops, formed a guard of honor along Westminster Street for Veterans of past wars that marched in the parade.

During the week of June 25 to July 2, 1911, the troop, invited by the Third Providence Troop, attended the first summer camp devoted exclusively to Scouting. The expedition was held on the eastern side of Prudence Island. A major highlight of the week was the transmission of the first electrical message (wireless transmission) ever dispatched from the Island. The troops met at Union Station for the train ride to Bristol and subsequent transport to Prudence Island.

In June 1916, Camp Yawgoog officially opened with the First Providence Troop helping to inaugurate the camp. Approximately 15 Scouts left Exchange Place (Kennedy Plaza) with all Scouts riding the distance standing in the back of a truck. Nightly ghost stories and initiations were enjoyed by all. The first meal at Yawgoog under a Grey Arbor was complicated by insects dropping into the food and drink with many jokes thereafter referring to the name "bug juice".

The approach of World War I was bringing to the Boy Scouts of America government recognition, so that in May, 1917, the Rhode Island Boy Scouts, including the First Providence Troop, voted to merge and become the Greater Providence Council, Boy Scouts of America. The past Scout members were recognized.

The First Providence Troop is proud to say that "we still have the first flag from 1917". The troop also participated in the parade at the conclusion of the war. During the reign of John McPherson, Jr. as Scoutmaster, the troop annually donated food baskets at Thanksgiving, collected clothes for the poor, repaired and collected toys for children and actively participated in hikes and overnighters. Pioneers became the logo of the troop during this period. The troop in 1926 secured a 100-acre farm in Exeter, R.I. for a period of 10 years. During this time, a cabin was erected and financed by members of the troop.

In the 1970's, the troop was presented with proclamations from the Governor of Rhode Island and the Mayor of Providence for over 60 years of continuous service. Also, in the late 1970's, the troop moved from Broad Street School to Washington Park Community Center, with its new sponsor, the Washington Park Citizens Association. In the spring of 1990, the troop obtained new facilities and a new sponsor, Washington Park United Methodist Church. As a point of interest, the troop still exists in the same area, after these many years, within 500 feet from the original meeting place.

On August 25, 2000, Al DeCristo passed away after 42 years of service in Scouting to the troop. He is the only individual in the state to be awarded the Spirit of Scouting Award. During his lifetime, Al DeCristo influenced the lives of many boys on their trail to Eagle Scout and assisted them greatly. Other notable leaders of the First Providence Troop are Leonard E. Johnson, Herbert H. Boden, Jr., William "Wild Bill" A. Sandford, Henry 'Hank' and Phebe Vandersip—just to name a few. These great leaders worked hard to operate and maintain First Providence Troop for one hundred years.

During the past several years, we have participated in service projects such as Flag Ceremonies at the State House on Scout Sunday, the first Pasta Challenge at the State House, clean-up in Roger Williams Park on Emancipation Day and Grace Church Cemetery, Scouting for Food and being the Color Guard at the Heritage Festival Celebrations, just to name a few.

First Providence Troop Eagle Scouts

Rui Pedro Alves	01/01/92
John James Joseph Banks	01/19/95
Phillip David Alexander Banks	01/01/98
John Patrick Beaton	11/08/73
Richard Bowen	07/27/26
Timothy N. Buffum	08/24/39
William M. Burke	06/18/71
Roy Dailey	07/03/72
Antonio C. Dias	07/01/04

Joshua Fitzgerald	06/16/05
Nathan Antone Flores	06/16/05
John D. Gaskell	12/14/57
Randy Theodore Hansen	07/01/04
Clinton Johnson	04/20/31
David Lamb	12/22/71
Glenn Lee Martin	01/18/73
Gary Noel McNally	01/30/03
Daniel McOsker	02/07/74
John McPherson	04/01/27
Manny Medeiros	05/03/94
Charles W. Morgan	04/17/67
Hugh P. O'Shaughnessy	11/25/50
John Pliakas	08/16/53
William A. Sandford	08/29/30
Edison Osiris Santana	12/06/93
Arthur B. Schweikart	09/30/25
William Taylor	12/22/71

TROOP 1 WAKEFIELD

The Troop was being organized in late 1910 as a RIBS Troop. Records from the Committee Chair, Simon Wreschinsky, who served in this position from 1911 through 1938, are still intact. At that time he was honored by the National Council as being the oldest, and longest serving leader at that time in the U.S. It was his 27th year of service, and he was in his 80's. The troop has been chartered by the South Kingstown Lions Club for over 65 years. Grafton I. Kenyon was the first Scoutmaster, and served until 1915.

The Troop has been meeting in a cabin off Silver Lake Avenue that they have owned since 1939. It was being built during 1938, but was partially destroyed by the Hurricane of 1938 before it was completed.

The Troop also had a Sea Scout Patrol during 1939, for the older scouts.
Troop 1 frequently hiked to summer camp at Yawgoog during earlier times, taking two days to get there.

The Troop donated a bronze bell to Camp Yawgoog shortly before World War II. It is still in use to this day in the Camp Three Point to mark noon, and the minute of silence as all Scouts and leaders pause to remember those Scouts that have served, and died for God and Country.

Troop 1 Wakefield Eagle Scouts

Aseef Hassan Ahmed	03/07/07
Benjamin Hettrick Berry	11/07/07
Christopher Aaron Berry	04/28/05
Robert Bitgood	05/03/89
Nicolas Andre Bossy	01/25/02
John F. Cameron	12/17/55
Dylan John Cashman	07/20/05
Scott R. Clancy	12/27/62
Robert Stephen Cruz, Jr.	12/13/10
David DeCubellis	12/27/62
James DeCubellis	12/27/62
Andrew M. Ferrigno	03/11/81
Michael Gobell	12/30/03
Stephen Neil Guarino	10/12/02
Erich Andrew Harvey	12/08/89
John E. Harvey, IV	07/21/88
John Hofford	08/27/42
Herbert M. Hofford, Jr.	04/23/49
Gary S. Johnson	03/20/86
Paul O. Johnson	10/17/83
John Joss	04/17/35
William Jennings Long, Jr.	11/04/03
William McNally, Jr.	04/17/35
Fred A. Michael, Jr.	12/01/60
Manual A.S. Morales	11/04/09
Sean A. Newton	04/16/08
Michael J. Poore	08/14/04
Neil Andrew Redmond	12/01/09
Joshua Perry Sargent	02/02/10
John R. Scattergood	07/30/59
Peter William Schofield, Jr.	09/19/88
Alec Silvestro	03/19/09
Michael K. Ulmschneider	01/26/83
Timothy A. Ulmschneider	04/28/87
William P. Ulmschneider	07/10/84
Frederick Wilson	08/30/55
Daniel David Woodford	11/20/97

TROOP 2 BRISTOL

Troop 2 Bristol at one of their many celebrations.

Originally sponsored by a Group of Citizens, their first charter was issued in April of 1919. The troop was then a member of the Greater Providence Council and met at the Boy Scout Building on Hope Street.

In 1930, when the council became the Narragansett Council, the troop was sponsored by the Bristol Lions Club, but continued to meet at the BS Building on Hope Street. Due to leadership issues, the Lions Club dropped sponsorship in 1938, but the troop continued, sponsored by the "American Citizens Committee". In 1940, sponsorship changed once again. Our Lady of Mount Carmel RC Church began sponsoring Troop 2, and the unit changed meeting location to the Parish Hall located on Congregational Street. In 1942, The Cup Defenders Association was approached to sponsor the unit after the pastor of the church stated that he was uninterested if the troop rechartered or not. The Cup Defender's Association secured leadership and a committee, but one by one, the leadership joined the military. The CDA never did officially sponsor the troop and the charter was dropped on April 26, 1943.

On November 1, 1952, the First Baptist Church of Bristol began chartering Troop 2 Bristol, and remains the chartering institution for the troop today.

Troop 2 Bristol Eagle Scouts

David S. Angell	04/30/66
Thomas E. Archibald	03/21/70
Nicholas Baker	03/22/04
Steven Baker	04/25/64
Leonard Baron	03/26/25
Nicholas P. Boisvert	06/30/94
Kyle E. Boyd	04/05/04
LeBaron Brown	10/19/22
Sheldon Burt	06/05/24
Barry Soares Carinha	01/08/02
Kurtis Michael Chubbuck	11/01/06
Herbert E. S. Clark III	02/01/74
Anthony M. Cordeiro	06/18/86
Jerry D. Cornman	04/29/67
Christopher Cox	10/09/04
Connor James Devin	09/23/10
Thomas Ensign DuBois	01/01/99
Timothy Ensign DuBois	03/12/02
Edward Dubois	12/16/03
Tyler DiSalvo Dubuc	01/04/11
Jamie L. Ervin	03/21/70
Frank Francis, Jr.	10/18/21
Thomas David Gallant	02/11/03
Craig S. Greene	09/23/75
Robert L. Heeks	02/01/67
William Heeks	04/24/65
Eric P. Labrie	09/24/03
Donald B. Lanoue	03/21/70
Patrick T. Lee	05/05/86
Joseph Lero	04/24/65
William Lero	04/17/35
Kevin W. Lombardi	10/03/79
Raymond C. Pagnano	09/14/63
Frank Perry	01/27/25
John Paul Perry	10/02/97
Richard A. Pimental, Jr.	04/03/97
George R. Popovici	01/13/76
Timothy Michael Pray	01/01/99

Paul Douglas Prindiville	03/05/06
Nicholas Ruggiero	10/18/23
Jerome D. Sanders	11/06/91
Peter Karl Sanders	08/19/94
Russell S. Serpa	08/05/04
Kevin R. Smith	05/24/05
Zachary Andrew St. Ours	02/06/08
Christopher W. Stanley	12/10/90
Brian Michael Sullivan	03/21/05
Thomas J. Sullivan	09/27/07
Michael B. Topazio	04/04/38
John B. Troiano, II	09/14/63
Brian Tucker	04/20/63
Harold E. Tucker	04/01/61
Thomas Twarog	09/14/63
Frank J. Twarog, Jr.	01/16/65
John Matthew Vittoria	04/29/03
Robert Vittoria	01/17/05
Joseph B. Vollaro	04/04/38
Kenneth E. Waters	04/12/04
George Nathan Webster	04/24/03
Craig W. Wilson	01/13/76
Matthew Gregory Wilson	06/13/06
Ronald E. Wilson	08/28/72
Scott R. Wilson	09/23/75

TROOP 2 EAST GREENWICH

The fall of 2010 marked the 88th anniversary of Troop 2 East Greenwich's founding. The idea for the troop originated with the Rev. Elmer West, newly arrived Pastor of the First Baptist Church in town. Pastor West proposed to the congregation, and it approved the formation of a new Boy Scout Troop, on September 27th, 1922. The Church received a Charter for the Troop on October 28th, 1922. The Rev. Mr. West served as the first Scoutmaster, with seven men of the church forming the first Scout committee. For the first six years, the troop met in the Swift Gym.

In 1927, the Rev. Mr. West left East Greenwich, soon after the Town's 250th Anniversary celebration that fall. The Troop played an active role in that celebration. Samuel Card became the new Scoutmaster. A year later, a third Scoutmaster took over, as the Troop also acquired both a new sponsoring organization, American Legion Post 15, and a new home, the "Scout House" on Spring Street. Troop 2 continues to meet here today, 80 plus years later.

On November 1st, 1932, Frank Mellor became Scoutmaster. He would serve a distinguished tenure of just over 13 years, until his death on December 30th, 1945. Through the '20's, '30's and '40's, the Troop was very active in community service efforts, in addition to its typical Scout hiking and camping events. In 1925 and 1926, the Troop helped the town with its cleanup days. In the '30's and '40's the troop distributed clothing, food baskets, and toys the Scouts repaired, to those in need at holiday time. During World War II and beyond, the Troop collected aluminum cans, newspapers, magazines, and more, for the war effort. While Mr. Mellor was Scoutmaster, the Scouts constructed patrol dens in the basement of the Scout Hall. Seventeen boys became Eagle Scouts under his leadership.

Richard T. Proctor served as Scoutmaster, after service in World War II, from 1946 until mid-1949. The Troop suffered its one regrettable incident during this time. In August 1945, the Troop's older Scouts, in a panel truck they had refurbished, traveled to New Hampshire to camp and go mountain climbing. On the return trip, the truck collided with a bus, resulting in the death of one Scout, John Lincoln Nichols. Troop 2 continues to this day to honor his memory with a memorial service at his grave each May. From 1949 to 1956, several men served as Scoutmaster, including George Halsband, Donald S. Houghton, and Maynard Bennett. In February of 1956 the Troop began its tradition of an annual dinner, which continues to today.

A very dynamic period for the Troop was that of 1956 through 1962, when Raymond T. Dunphy served as Scoutmaster, closely assisted by Stanley S. Andersen. During this period Troop sponsorship changed (after about 30 years with the American Legion Post 15) to local manufacturer, Bostitch, Inc., who would also serve in this role for about 30 years. In July 1959, the 131st Toronto, Canada Troop spent two weeks in Rhode Island, including one week with Troop 2 at Yawgoog. Ten years later Troop 2 would reconnect with some of the same Canadian leadership, now with the 7th Thornhill Troop (in greater Toronto), for a similar exchange. In each case, Troop 2 would journey to Toronto in the following summer for two weeks, staying in boys homes, but for one week, camping with their Canadian Scout hosts at the Haliburton Scout Reserve.

In September of 1965 Jim Essex became Scoutmaster, following George Sargent, Paul R. Friend, and Francis Roy. Under Mr. Friend the Troop hiked the 50-mile Long Trail in Northern New England. Under Mr. Roy the Troop started a five year stretch of a week long summer encampment on the Gatineau River, in Quebec, Canada (1965-1969). In the 45 plus years of Mr. Essex's tenure as Scoutmaster, the Troop has revisited Canada at least five times, including that second exchange venture with the 7th Thornhill Troop in 1959 and 1960. Favorite Canadian city destinations have been Montreal and Quebec City. Among American cities visited (most at least several times) are: New York City, Philadelphia, Washington DC, the historic Virginia triangle of Jamestown, Williamsburg, and Yorktown, and of course,

Boston, MA. The Troop has continued its community service efforts, today regularly taking part in Scouting for Food in the fall, the Inner City Churches Soup Kitchen in Providence each winter (until 2009), replaced by the local Community Dinner in East Greenwich on the last Monday of each month (in 2010), regularly marches in town parades honoring our military, each May flags RI Veterans Cemetery (has done so since the cemetery was established in the 1970's), the Town's Earth Day in April, and more.

In 1987 and 1988 Troop 2 Scout's took part in an international exchange program with Scouts in Coventry, England. In 1999 Troop 2 Scouts traveled to Leicestshire, England for an exchange with the 2nd Quorn Scout Group, which visited Rhode Island for about two weeks in the summer of 2000. In February, 2008 two Troop 2 Scouts, Chris Capuano and Kevin Drumm, were part of a Narragansett Council contingent traveling to the Dominican Republic for about eight days.

Thanks to a bequest by Senator G. Elsworth Gale some years ago, the Troop has a special fund to assist older Scouts in attending the Philmont Scout Ranch in Cimmaron, New Mexico each summer.

The Troop continues to sell wreaths each November-December to help finance its programs and equipment needs. The current sponsor of Troop 2 is the East Greenwich Boys Home Association, which owns the hall the Troop uses. It is made up of local citizens interested in supporting youth programs in town.

Since its founding in the fall of 1922, Troop 2 has had 181 (as of March 1, 2011) boys attain the rank of Eagle Scout, the highest award a boy can earn in the Boy Scouts of America. When Jim Essex became Scoutmaster in 1965, some 48 boys had attained that rank.

The list of **Eagle Scouts from Troop 2 East Greenwich** follows.

Roy A. Card	01/05/28	Jordan S. Abrams	12/04/39
Cheslie Carpenter	04/15/29	James Cheever	05/03/43
William Clegg	04/15/29	Glenn H. King	08/26/43
Edward J. Keenan	04/15/29	M. Russell Leyden	05/03/43
Harold Meller	04/15/29	David R. Nichols	12/27/43
Ambrose Reisert	04/15/29	George G. Anderson, Jr.	12/16/44
James Bertwell	04/05/37	Richard T. Proctor	08/21/47
John G. Byrne	04/05/37	Peter Ballou	08/18/49
Otto Wilhelm Olson, Jr.	04/05/37	Paul R. Cheever	11/26/49
Thomas D. Reisert	04/05/37	Bruce E. Fogel	08/18/49
Maynard Bennett	04/04/38	Michael A. Malvinni	08/24/50

David Bergstrom	04/04/38	Craig W. Clarke	12/27/52
Charles Bertwell	04/04/38	Frederick L. Hurd	08/17/52
Thomas H. Byrnes	04/04/38	David C. Norman	12/27/52
William Henry	04/04/38		
Everett Lundberg	04/04/38		
Ralph S. Madison	04/04/38		
John A. Reisert	12/27/52	Michael A. Copotosta	04/15/83
James F. Springfield	12/27/52	Michael J. Davis	09/28/82
Richard McGraw, Jr.	03/27/54	Kenneth B. Knox	09/28/82
Robert P. Hammond	12/17/55	Paul S. Nanian	12/28/82
Reeves W. Westmoreland	12/17/55	Peter A. St. Godard	06/02/83
Roger Cady	05/01/56	Andrew R. Lemoi	10/15/84
Albert J. Cote, III	08/04/56	Graham Stevens	11/22/83
Edward Kovac	12/31/58	Robert F. Calvano	07/15/85
Kevin Dunphy	12/12/59	Kevin J. Turner	08/08/85
Raymond Cellemme	08/13/61	Stephen E. Verrier	08/08/85
Kenneth E. Knox	04/01/61	Andrew R. Vineyard	07/12/85
James Kovac	04/01/61	Shawn M. Witt	02/14/85
Robert Mitchell	04/01/61	James V. Calvano	05/05/86
Robert A. Knox	11/20/63	E. Stefan Coutoulakis	01/17/86
Stephen Moore	08/12-63	Mark A. Kenyon	08/14/86
Nicols Littlefield, Jr.	09/28/67	John A. Lutfy	07/16/86
Daniel R. McClure	02/21/67	Mark D. Sicco	04/15/85
Ernest G. Zielinski	06/16/69	James F. Holbrook	02/13/87
Edward A. Tomasi	12/14/70	Andrew H. Davis	04/08/88
Kevin M. Clement	05/10/71	Blake Gunnar Svendsen	12/15/88
Jeffrey Plouffe	08/28/72	Christopher C. Capotosto	06/30/89
Steven Wilson	03/30/72	Todd Jeffrey LaLonde	06/29/89
Stephen Brown	01/23/73	Robert Joseph Tingle, Jr.	09/11/89
Charles M. Dickerson	01/23/73	Elias J. Deeb	04/12/90
John Michael Falvey	09/10/73	James Thomas Doyle, Jr.	08/10/90
John Payne	01/23/73	Craig Andrew Lundsten	08/10/90
Stephen Smith	01/23/73	Christian E. Smith	10/09/90
Chad Hoffmeister	01/30/74	Phillipss H. Hart Hinch	03/05/91
Timothy J. Smith	01/23/74	Douglas C.	
Brian T. Hatch	01/27/75	MacGunnigle, II	11/12/91
Kevin J. McDonogh	01/27/75	Brian A. Budlong	01/10/92
Lloyd L. Beale, Jr.	03/05/76	Paul J. Choquette, III	05/07/92
James J. Leach	03/04/76	Kurt Joseph Kazlauskas	09/17/92
Jeffrey R. Nylund	02/14/77	Christopher A. Lisy	07/16/92
Bernard L. Patenaude	02/14/77	John Brendan Newman	01/01/92
Jeffrey S. Carver	03/09/78	Jeffry T. Ross	03/16/93

David J. Dickerson	06/05/78	Jonathan Kyle Hecker	02/08/94
Richard Dietz	03/09/78	Kevin Antaya Kazlauskas	08/25/94
Neil S. Day	04/10/79	Christopher M. Lundsten	01/01/94
Thomas E. Day	04/10/79	Christopher J. Cawley	02/09/95
Steven C. Sidel	05/22/79	Frederick W. Lumb	04/27/95
John J. Gallogly	01/05/80	James Michael	
Stephen P. Holbrook	05/29/81	Robinson Sloan	03/09/95
Andrew J. St. Godard	03/11/81	John Thomas Walsh, III	11/14/95
Stephen B. Tingle	05/12/81	Matthew V. Cawley	10/10/96
Stephen J. Carll	06/03/82	Matthew Lundsten	06/11/96
Steve Case	01/01/82	Derrick James Mong	10/10/96
John K. Nanian	01/12/82	William Robert Sequino	11/07/96
Joseph C. VanDeWater	12/16/81		
Brian P. Clement	09/28/82		
J. David C.M.Whittingham	09/19/96	Philip Wooley Young	04.27/04
Matthew Wolcott	05/16/96	Marc Paul Capuano	09/14/05
Brian Matthew Lehrman	07/08/97	Justin A. Fox	01/27/05
Andrew R. Lumb	12/09/97	Alexander John Hiller	10/24/05
David Lee Zelinski	04/21/97	Michael V. MacAndrew	04/28/05
Matthew Hayes Parker	01/01/98	Eric M. Spain	12/22/05
Eric Alan Rice	01/01/98	Justin R. Vespia	08/02/05
William F. Robinson, III	01/01/98	Richard J. Casey, III	10/24/06
Jason Thomas Rankin	01/01/99	Joshua M. Kenyon	12/12/06
Jordan Michael Schibler	01/01/99	Ross Francis MacAndrew	09/07/06
Daniel John Cummings	01/01/00	Praveen Simha Murthy	09/07/06
Victor Hoi-Foung Ng	03/09/00	David Matthew Nunez	09/07/06
Philip George Kazlauskas	11/29/01	Alexander K. Schaller	06/08/06
James Alan Russell, Jr.	11/25/01	Andrew Rowe Treat	10/24/06
Eric James Schweikart	12/13/01	Christopher J. Capuano	09/18/07
Todd Robert Harrison	10/24/02	Jonathan C. Lamantia	04/23/07
Jason Michael Pare	08/10/02	Benjamin E. Lovejoy	05/15/07
Joseph Frederick Laforge	11/04/03	Andrew Austin Croll	10/27/08
Christopher Longenbaker	02/12/03	Kyle John Kenyon	08/13/08
William C. Maloney	03/26/03	Nishant N. Shah	02/12/08
Theodore S. Parker	12/23/03	Kevin Longfellow Drumm	10/20/09
Thomas Briggs Pritchard	12/04/03	Bryce Joseph MacAndrew	08/05/09
Connor L. Smith	07/30/03	Michael A. Cedrone	10/11/10
Matthew B. Albertsen	12/14/04	Vikram Simha Murthy	06/30/10
David Robert Bolton	04/27/04	Christopher John Ryan	01/28/10
Jason R. Essex	07.21/04		
Michael Mixer	01/05/04		
Austin Smith	10/07/04		

A major focus under Scoutmaster Essex has been the personal growth of each boy in citizenship training, leadership development, and acquiring a love of the outdoors through hiking, camping, and particularly more challenging activities like mountain climbing, canoeing, white water canoeing and rafting, and more. Character does count, and boys need to learn to be trustworthy, responsible, considerate, plus the other values found in the Scout Oath and Law. Here's to Troop 2, and its 88 years of service to the community, and to its youth!

CREW 2 SWANSEA

Crew 2 Swansea Hartwell Tavern

Sponsored by the 2nd Rhode Island Regiment of the Continental Army.

Venturing Crew 2 Swansea received its original charter on 7/1/09. The founding members are Carl Becker and Brian Jean. The unit members are drawn together by a love of history and war re-enactments.

History of the original 2nd RI Regiment of the Continental Army:

The 2nd Rhode Island Regiment camped and fought at the siege of Boston and at Quebec in 1775.
1776: at New York and Trenton
1777: at Princeton, Morristown, Fort Mercer, Fort Mifflin and Valley Forge
1778: at Monmouth and Rhode Island (Newport) and camps at Bristol and Warren, RI
1779: at Wickford, RI and Morristown, NJ
1780: at Springfield, NJ and Rhode Island Village, NY

In 1781, the 1st and 2nd Regiments combined and Col. Christopher Greene and others were lost at the massacre at Croton. The Rhode Islanders marched to Yorktown, VA where the Rhode Island Light Infantry led the redoubt assault. In 1782, they served in Philadelphia and West Point. In 1783, they marched again to Forts Herkimer and Oswego. The war ended and in 1784, the Rhode Island Regiment disbanded.

PACK 6 BRISTOL

The first charter for Pack 6 Bristol was issued on January 1, 1954. The unit has always been sponsored by St. Mary's RC Church, 330 Wood Street, Bristol, RI. The pack meets in the Parish Hall beneath the church and has no breaks in service since its first charter.

The Cubmasters of Pack 6 Bristol are listed below:

Melissa Medina	2009-		
Ian Chilcot	2006-2009	James Tavares	1985-1986
Victoria White	2003-2006	Kenneth Duckworth	1984-1985
Scott Donley	2002-2003	Jerome C. Sanders	1983-1984
Diane J. Cloutier	2000-2002	Richard Ferreira	1975-1983
Edward King	1998-2000	T. Matthew Clarke	1974-1975
Thomas Forsberg	1997-1998	Frank Liss	1971-1974
Bruce Ayres	1995-1997	John Greene	1968-1971
Robert Karsch	1993-1995	Edward Silvia	1967-1968
Roy Leffingwell	1991-1993	John Greene	1965-1967
Andrienne Camara	1990-1991	Andre Desaulniers	1964-1965
Patricia Cameron	1989-1990	Augustine Nerone	1955-1964
Mark Tucker	1986-1989	Joseph Gallagher	1954-1955

TROOP 6 BRISTOL

The first charter for Troop 6 Bristol was issued on October 25, 1939. The unit has always been sponsored by St. Mary's RC Church, 330 Wood Street, Bristol, RI. At that time, the troop met at St. Mary's School. The troop's last charter, before a break in service, expired in October of 1944, but officially dropped on September 23, 1946. A lack of leadership was cited as the reason for the unit's dissolution. On May 1, 1964, the troop was resurrected and once again sponsored by St. Mary's RC Church. The unit now meets in the Parish Hall beneath the church.

Troop 6 Bristol Eagle Scouts

John J. Anderson-O'Flaherty	01/13/09
Geoffrey B. Avila	05/19/94
Bradley Joseph Ayres	01/11/11
Matthew Bruce Ayres	01/14/03
Christopher McCarthy Azar	02/26/08
Charles E. Belmore	03/30/80
Mark Bettencourt	05/22/03
Ronald George Blanchard	10/23/08
Paul Breault	09/10/02
Edward Roy Broderick	09/05/86
Charles A. Burke	09/22/70
Jason S. Caetano	07/19/00
David J. Cairrao	11/29/83
Timothy P. Calandra	07/22/84
Christopher Michael Cameron	01/01/98
Steven James Capuano	12/18/02
Stephen A. Cross	08/15/83
Jason P. DeRobbio	01/01/99
Nicholas J. Deveau	03/30/04
Christopher F. DiMaio	06/19/79
Matthew Stephenson Donley	01/20/04
Brian Michael Dutra	12/17/09
Peter Michael Ferreira	09/02/08
Brian Thomas Forsberg	02/11/03
Marc Christopher Gallant	06/05/07
Jared Arthur Gardiner	04/21/06
Glenn S. Greene	08/10/77
Douglas Roscoe Hendrix	01/11/11
Philip S. Johnson	07/11/06
Joshua Edward King	03/19/09
Bryan Leffingwell	09/20/01
William F. Lombardi	01/20/84
Nicolas Rafael Mariscal	03/18/08
Robert A. Martin	08/30/72
Vincent P. Micheletti	03/23/84
Benjamin J. Murray	02/08/01
Raymond B. Murray, Jr.	02/29/96
Gary A. Paul	10/28/83

Adam Pimenta	04/30/02
Kyle James Porto	02/11/10
Marc Rabideau	08/17/10
Shane Reynolds	05/10/05
Richard R. Reynolds, Jr.	02/11/03
Anthony Valentine Rocha, MD	05/03/68
Joseph Louis Silvia, Jr.	02/11/10
Kevin Ryan Spencer	04/27/10
David G. St. Germain	06/14/85
Justin Paul Teixeira	10/25/05
Trent D. Theroux	04/09/86
Peter Shakley Van Siclen	09/27/01
Heath L. Ver Burg	08/10/89
Jeffrey L. VerBurg, Jr.	02/26/88
Kenneth R. Walmsley	02/05/82
Mason Taylor Wetherald	10/30/07
Connor Francis White	08/11/10
James Robert Wright	02/17/00

TROOP 6 CRANSTON

Mary Lou Kavanaugh of the Cranston Herald tells of her father Edward Fitzgerald, who wished to start a Boy Scout troop in Cranston in the 1920's. He approached Father Thomas Tiernan, the pastor at St. Ann's Church in Knightsville from 1918-1933, with the idea. Father Tiernan was not obliged to have it there because it was not endorsed by the Roman Catholic Church. He recommended that the boys join catholic youth groups, according to the printed copy of Troop 6's history, *The Best By Far*, compiled by Robert A. Carnevale, M.D. In 1935, The Catholic Bishop of the Providence Diocese, Bishop Keough, endorsed the Boy Scouts. St. Ann's would later become the sponsor of Troop 6 in 2001.

At that time, there weren't any Boy Scout Troops in the Meshanticut section of Cranston. As a central spot in the city for recreation near the artificially created lake, an elementary school on Curtis Street and the church and fire station, many community reformers were looking for youth programming for the children.

The vicar at the church, Rev. Mr. Albert Cecil Larned, had come back to Rhode Island in 1923 after being ordained a deacon and later a priest in England and serving as the Dean at All Saints' Cathedral in Albany. Larned, and three community leaders, James Bolan, George Wellington and G. Frank Balcom, came together to plan having a Boy Scout Troop at St. David's, located at 1951 Cranston Street, the first Scouting unit in Cranston. Rev. Larned was the first Scoutmaster.

Antonio "Jock" Maggiacomo moved from Italy to be with his family, who found work in Warren. His family was from the mountain village of Itri and because many of his townspeople lived in Knightsville, his family moved to that part of Cranston in 1923. He had been a member of the Boy Scouts while living in Warren and was a Yawgoog veteran. He joined Troop 6 and later went on to be a well known figure in Cranston. He opened a lemonade shop on Park Avenue and played for the local baseball team. He coached baseball and football and taught personal fitness to the Scouts from Troop 6 well after his Scouting days were over.

By 1926, according to *The Best By Far,* Rev. Larned stepped down as scoutmaster and moved to St. Margaret's Church in Brighton, Mass. A new executive staff member, Dana "Dan" Lamb, became Scoutmaster of the troop and instilled a lot of outdoor skills, such as tracking, hunting and wilderness survival, in the mostly urban youth. A tract of land in the city, called Skeleton Valley, was used by the Scouts for camping and instruction, which is where Lamb had done much of his teaching. He left in 1927 and turned the position over to Leslie Whiting, a World War I veteran.

Whiting stayed on as Scoutmaster of the troop during the Great Depression, but the relationship with St. David's Church faded. Two more community leaders in the city, City Councilman George Bennett and Arthur Crompton, were determined to keep Scouting in the village, and they helped reserve the Community Hall next to the Curtis Street fire station as the new meeting place. The Depression would eventually take its toll, and Whiting needed to find work and stepped down as Scoutmaster in 1930.

They found 24-year-old George Udell to take over and he served in that role from 1930-1933. He used skills he learned in the National Guard to teach the boys and get them involved with outdoor activities. He later would fight in World War II and rose to the rank of Lt. Colonel in the U.S. Army. The troop had moved to the fire station where Udell's son, George, was Senior Patrol Leader. The new Scoutmaster was Bill Sandford. *The Best By Far* describes Scouting as getting better despite the Depression.

Campouts were potluck. One boy would go to the meat market to get soup bones for free. The scouts would bring vegetables from the garden, a potato out of a home larder, maybe on a good night 15 cents of boiling beef and put the collection in a same pot for all to enjoy. Parts of the Boy Scout uniform were recycled among the neighborhood boys because few would afford a new uniform.

The troop began its stay at the Meschanticut Community Center, where the "Tot Park" is today, from 1930 until 1978. It was during this period that Troop 6 began to grow and became a familiar part of the neighborhood. Their fun and success was confined to the area until some boys from the troop made state-wide headlines. James "Bud" Heaton, Clement McPhee, Irving Smith, Gilbert Daniels and James Lord were swimming in Meschanticut Lake and saw a young man, Frank White, of Providence beginning to drown. Lord dove into the lake to rescue the boy and brought his unconscious body up from the bottom of the water. They were all able to get him into their canoe and gave him "artificial" respiration. He was revived and the Scouts were awarded for saving White's life.

There were other heroes during this period, including Ben Riley, whose father Ben was also Scoutmaster. He was able to retrieve a drifting row boat at Yawgoog that had Chief William's young daughter inside and was praised by Williams and asked to dine with him at the Chief's table at dinner. The Bennet family of the troop became world class athletes, including Bob Bennett, who won a Bronze Medal in track and field at the 1948 Olympic Games in London, and Sky Bennett, who went on to play professional baseball in the Boston Red Sox organization.

The troop also began looking into different areas to camp and swim, including Warwick Downs and participating in the Council Jamboree at the Rhode Island Auditorium. The troop also began being more successful in the Depression Era in advancing its Scouts, as seen in William Cumerford, who became Troop 6 Cranston's first Eagle Scout on August 13, 1933 at Yawgoog. Soon after, on August 30, 1935, Earl Crompton was became the second Eagle Scout. He also worked at Yawgoog as a bugler and later as waterfront director at Three Point.

Cumerford, known as "the snake man" for his ability with tying knots, made a career of Scouting. He became a scout executive in upstate New York and became talented at fundraising. He helped in developing the Yawgoog Alumni Association in the 1980's and helped in fundraising efforts for improvements to the camp.

A local paperboy, Lawrence Barrett, was the troop's next Eagle in 1939. He was very active in the troop but was devoted to his paper route, so he did not do any extracurricular activities other than Scouting until college. It was at Rhode Island State College in South Kingstown, where he took Mechanical Engineering and was able to harness an ability to run. He made the Cross Country Team and helped lead them to the 1941 and 1942 New England Championship. He was named to the University of Rhode Island Athletic Hall of Fame in 1996.

He joined Westinghouse in 1943 and designed and developed jet engines and continued in that line of work until his retirement in 1987. He spent from 1957-1987 with Vertol Company (now part of Boeing) designing helicopters.

Many of the boys of Troop 6 joined in the military during World War II in this period, including George Udell, who earned the Distinguished Service Cross.

A former Scout and Troop 6 Scoutmaster, Ken Potter, earned the Distinguished Service Cross, two Purple Hearts, a Bronze Star, a Silver Star and a Presidential Citation for his bravery and valor while serving the U.S. Army in Northern Africa. He, too, was a member of the URI Athletic Hall of Fame after being captain of the football and baseball teams. Potter is buried in Arlington National Cemetery. His brother, Ralph Potter, first was a member of Troop 6 and would then join the Sea Scouts. He became an All-American in sailing and joined the Coast Guard during the war. He participated in the Blood Winter Convoy Campaign in 1943 and, after the war, taught sailing skills in multiple organizations. He was President of Potter Hazelhurtst, Inc. and CEO of Makeira Marketing.

Troop 6, along with the other Boy Scouts from the Council, were involved in assisting our country during World War II. They collected aluminum cans and newspapers for recycling, assist the Red Cross in disaster drills and helped distribute war related literature and posters. At the end of the war in 1945, a new era began for the troop, which included a new Scoutmaster.

32-year-old William Sandford, an Eagle Scout, became Scoutmaster and held the position longer than any Scoutmaster in the troop's history. He moved the troop from camping at Three Point at Yawgoog to campsite Kit Carson in the new Sandy Beach subcamp. The Troop's first African-American Scout, William White, joined at this time. He later would become a Cranston Police officer. The troop would form a rivalry with Troop 4 Cranston and competed in swimming, knot tying, baseball games and other activities. The troop camped a great deal at a campground called Skeleton Valley, which is now Champlin Scout Reservation. Sandford left the troop in 1954 to serve in a variety of volunteer roles with the Narragansett Council but was instrumental in helping the troop to return to St. David's Church in 1978. He earned the distinguished Silver Beaver award later in 1955.

The 1950's saw an active troop as well as its first Eagle Scout since Larry Barrett earned the distinction in 1939. Thomas Ciccone became the troop's fourth Eagle Scout on August 30, 1950. He later became involved in the construction industry and was a Scoutmaster for a local troop. It was in 1951 when Troop 6 went international as it helped collect clothing for overseas relief in a nationwide project under the direction of the United Nations. That same year, the troop's top cook, Augustus Tagliaferri, became an Eagle Scout. He later joined the U.S. Army and graduated from the University of Missouri Dental School. He joined on as a volunteer with the San Fernando Valley Council in California. He left the business of dentistry to became a business and investment advisor.

Sandford asked a former Scout from Troop16 at St. Mary's Church, Frank Mancini, to become Scoutmaster in 1954. Mancini stayed on until 1956. The troop helped clear land in Coventry for a camping area, and they began to spend more time doing Scout activities there and in areas of Knightsville. Mancini's sister, Lucy Mancini Ciccarelli, made a career of Scouting as she was the registrar for the Narragansett Council for 34 years. Upon Frank Mancini's departure, Sandford helped find a new Scoutmaster and asked friend Harry Sunderland, a police officer.

Sunderland continued to bring the Scouts outside and had a lot of physical activities done at a gravel pit where Cranston West High School now sits. He brought a police officer's discipline to the troop dynamic, which had a lasting impression. He retired from public service in 1982 and was honored by the city in 1987. Sunderland left the troop in 1960 and, with 36 boys, they needed a new leader. One of the boys' fathers, G. Howard Curtis, stepped up. He became the first father of a Troop 6 scout to be Scoutmaster. An avid hiker, he led the troop on many outdoor excursions, including moving the troop from Kit Carson at Yawgoog to campsite Paul Siple.

The troop began to meet at Champlin Scout Reservation more often and used it as a home away from home. The troop lashed branches together to create towers throughout the camp as well as bridges. Pioneering became a trademark of the troop as Curtis was an engineer by trade. Rank advancement became more commonplace, and four Eagles earned the award on June 17, 1964: Richard and John Sandberg, Kenny Manni and John Corrigan. Both Sandbergs became Mormons and attended Brigham Young University. They became involved as leaders with various Scouting units chartered with the Church of Latter Day Saints during their adult lives. They also both became engineers.

Manni also became involved in Scouting as an adult and volunteered for the Mount Baker Council. He also volunteered for the Franciscan Sisters and Benedictine Monastery in addition to having a general law practice in Oak Harbor, Washington. His sons Nathan and David would become Eagle Scouts 40 years later.

Curtis led a vibrant troop until he died during a Scout function on May 4, 1967 while the boys were clearing weeds as a community service project. He stated to assistant J. Edward Howarth that he did not feel well and then collapsed. The Scouts were able to get helped from the nearby fire department, but he could not be revived. The tragedy was shocking for the troop, and they needed a new leader. Howarth stepped forward to take over as Scoutmaster and would be their leader for 21 years. A decorated World War II veteran, Howarth continued on the troop's traditions. Both of his sons, David and Jim Howarth, earned the rank of Eagle Scout and went on to serve our country in the U.S. Armed Forces.

The troop flourished for two decades under Howarth's stewardship. He earned the Silver Beaver Award but in 1985, at the age of 69, he passed away after years of serving Troop 6 as the Scoutmaster and a committee member. Two Scouts during his tenure, Eagle Scouts Gene Emery and John Morrocco, took a path away from the confines of Cranston and into the world of news gathering. Emery was a reporter for the Providence Journal and the Health and Science Editor and Morrocco was a reporter for Defense News and contributing editor for Aviation Weekly and Space Technology. He also was a Pentagon Correspondent and worked for Boeing. They earned their Eagle in 1968 along with Jack Gustafson and Rick Sharp. Gustafson had a career in computers at AMICA, Leesona, Fatima Hospital and Blue Cross. Sharp made a career of photography, including a stint with Rolling Stone.

Another Eagle, Mark Scott, attended Brown University Medical School and was the camp doctor at Yawgoog. Howarth stepped down as Scoutmaster in 1971. With no leader and a changing social dynamic surrounding the War in Vietnam, the troop dwindled down to 11 boys. Neil Scott became an Eagle Scout on November 11, 1972, but the troop had less structure and much of the advancement was earned individually. The sponsor, Meshanticut Fire Station, looked for help and reached out to Bill Sandford. He recruited an 18-year old from Troop 3 Providence, Ed Rainone, to lead Troop 6. Rainone was embraced at the troop and brought a new era for the troop. They started with eight boys, and he quickly brought the group back to life.

The troop did a great deal of activities such as camping out at Camp Buxton in Rehoboth and Fort Getty in Jamestown, going to the Civic Center to see the Rhode Island Reds play hockey and wrestling shows, beach days at Gaspee Point and other new adventures. The troop's first female registered leader, Carol Sylvia, joined the troop as a committee member in 1973. The troop also celebrated 50 years at the fire station. While at Troop 3, Rainone had been a part of a unit that was very competitive with other troops. He brought that mentality to Troop 6, and they developed a friendly rivalry with Troop 99 in Federal Hill. They challenged each other at Yawgoog in many activities. In 1976, the troops were continuing a boxing tradition when one of the competitors injured himself and was brought to the Health Lodge. A court case went later in front of the Rhode Island Supreme Course in regards to liability. The ruling found that the participant was at fault, but that ended boxing at Yawgoog. That same year saw Rainone's last year as Scoutmaster. He had overseen three boys make Eagle: Dave Lamantia, Bruce Elam and Jim Kalashian.

In 1977, the fire station was slated for demolition. That ended the troop's 50-year relationship with the community center and fire station. A playground was to be built in its place. New Scoutmaster Mike DeLuca, who was an assistant under Rainone, looked to the committee for a new sponsor. Old sponsor St. David's had moved to Meshanticut Valley Parkway and welcomed the troop back. Ed Kdonian became the first Eagle Scout under DeLuca's leadership.

Like Rainone, DeLuca continued to find new activities for the boys to do. They went horseback riding, swam at the Wanskuck Boys and Girls Club, camping at Camp Richard, biking, body surfing in Nantucket and more. When other troops were struggling with membership, Troop 6 Cranston had 36 boys and 16 adults registered in 1979. The boys and leaders in the troop had established a strong bond, which helped them succeed and grow through this period. DeLuca left as Scoutmaster and Jim Vartanian took over in 1982. He continued the troop's adventurous spirit in the 1980's and planned trips to Maine, canoe trips through Baxter State park and a great deal more. Vartanian returned to active military service in 1991 and would help DeLuca and Kdonian start Troop 8 Cranston in the western part of the city later on. Adults such as Scott Salibury, DeLuca, Jim Kalasian, Jack Caldwell and Kdonian brought a youthful spirit to the ranks but Vartanian had to stepped down as Scoutmaster in 1986. St. David's and the troop looked to some help from the Council, and Sandford and district commissioner Frank Ferraro found someone right for the position.

Owen McDermott was signing his sons up for Scouting, and he was asked to take on the position, which he led for five years. He developed a boys leading boys strategy, and the troop continued to flourish. He was go on to earn the Silver Beaver Award. The troop began camping on the Simmons Reservoir on land owned by a Scout's family. That land is now part of the Central Landfill. Scott McGeough became the first Eagle that McDermott would have in 1986, and there would be more, including David and Mark Williams, Joseph, John and Steve Arcand, Brick Zawislak, Mike Joubert, Anthony Gallo, Bob Lesuer, Ryan Riccio and Larry Fagan. The troop became active in community events such as road races and participated in Scout Sunday at the church and in the Scouting for Food drive.

The 1990's saw another new era with a new Scoutmaster and committee chair. McDermott recruited his cousin, Frank Ferraro, who was crossing his son over from the pack to the troop and had experience as a Scoutmaster in Johnston. He also had been a District Chairman. Dave Turgeon would become the committee chair. They bought new gear, instituted new budgeting strategies to help with their fundraising and began new outdoor excursions, such as Lake Umbagog in New Hampshire. Dave Libby, a U.S. Marshall and committee member, was able to get access to special tours of the White House, FBI and The Pentagon in Washington, D.C. The troop saw President Bill Clinton at Arlington National Cemetery and attended a Washington Redskins football game. The troop grew to around 50 boys and began to outgrow the area designated for them at St. David's. Still sponsored by the church, they moved their meetings to Glen Hills School in 1994. A new pastor would be instituted soon after and the troop moved its meetings back. Troop 6 continued to camp at Campsite Paul Siple at Yawgoog until 2000 when it moved to both the new site Neil Armstrong and the existing site John Glenn, still at subcamp Sandy Beach.

The troop sent many boys to the National Jamboree in Virginia in 1993 and many held leadership positions. One boy, David Carnevale, became the troop's first Scout to attend at World Jamboree in 1999 in Chile. 32 boys earned Eagle under Ferraro's oversight, and Troop 6 had made its mark on Scouting in Cranston. It moved its sponsorship to St. Ann's Church to accommodate its special needs. Many adults have taken on district and Council volunteer positions.

Eagle Scouts from Troop 6 Cranston

Kyle Agronick	03/19/09
John Kenneth Anderson	08/09/05
John Arcand	12/15/93
Joseph J. Arcand	10/20/88
Stephen J. Arcand	05/24/90
Nathan Peter Baillargeon	04/09/08
Lawrence D. Barrett, Jr.	03/27/39
Devin Scott Blau	08/15/07
Jerry Maurica Blau	03/12/10
Jeffrey Kachig Boghossian, Jr.	01/30/08
Benjamin J. Caito	07/11/95
Nicholas J. Caramadre	04/06/05
Daniel Thor Carlson	10/17/01
Hans W. Carlson	10/27/04
David Frank Carnevale	01/01/98
Joseph Carnevale	08/11/04
Robert John Carnevale	04/11/01
Thomas Ciccone	08/24/50
Robert Norman Clark	10/15/09
Anthony James Conard	12/12/01
Stephen A. Conard	05/28/03
John Corrigan	09/12/64
Michael Raymond Creta	08/15/07
Earle W. Crompton	09/30/34
William R. Cumerford	08/31/33
Jonathan Nelson Danho	03/28/01
Daniel Michael DeGrandpre	05/09/07
Matthew K. DeGrandpre	08/11/04
Nicholas A. DeNardo	10/04/06
Michael Richard Derderian	12/18/08
Jason Paul Dias	04/19/00

Steven J. Dispirito	06/03/82
Devon Robert Dubuque	02/12/09
Patrick O'Neil Durigan	04/06/06
Bruce H. Elam	07/02/75
Matthew Eugene Emery	01/01/98
Chesley Eugene Emery, Jr.	02/22/68
Schuyler William English	05/29/07
Lawrence Joseph Fagan	01/01/92
Dylan Thomas Farley	05/13/10
Michael Frank Ferraro	05/22/96
Timothy John Flannery	12/17/09
Aaron Brandon French	03/01/06
Eric Jared French	05/10/01
Alexander Todd Gaines	10/04/06
Benjamin C. Gaines	05/28/03
Zachary Robert Gaines	08/12/08
Michael P. Gallo	08/26/96
Anthony Louis Gallo, Jr.	03/13/91
Anthony Paul Genco	05/09/07
Daniel Pasquale Genco	09/16/10
Trevor James Gerard	10/27/04
Andrew Joseph Ginsberg	05/22/02
Jeffrey Simone Girard, III	05/10/01
Joseph Girardi	09/27/08
William John Greenaway	08/09/05
John A. Gustafson	05/02/68
Ryan James Hanley	12/12/01
Earl Nason Henry	02/18/87
David A. Howarth	10/25/67
James E. Howarth	05/14/66
James Jason Jaworski, Jr.	06/19/07
David Jeffrey	11/13/02
Timothy David Johnson	04/11/01
Michael Peter Joubert	06/29/94
James Kalashian	02/06/75
Derek Andrew Katznelson	03/14/07
Edward B. Kdonian	03/09/78
Daniel Adam Kittredge	01/01/99
Andrew John Kostrzewa	12/18/02
Daniel Paul Kostrzewa	07/12/05

Stephen Michael Kostrzewa	05/10/01
George Elias Koutros	08/12/08
David Lamantia	02/06/75
Nathan Lyle Landes	11/13/02
Gerard H. Larrivee, Jr.	03/21/67
Robert John LeSeur	12/16/90
Steven M. Lemos, Jr.	04/06/05
Michael W. Libby	08/28/96
Christopher Loens	12/10/03
Craig Malesra	04/28/04
Kyle Robert Malesra	10/27/01
Anthony J. Mangiarelli	07/11/95
Kenneth Manni	09/12/64
Joseph Frank Manzi	01/23/08
Andrew James Marrapese	10/21/10
Christopher Anthony McCartin	01/01/98
Scott P. McGeough	09/13/85
Mark James McPhillips	08/15/07
Ryan Douglas Miga	05/09/07
Matthew Miller	12/18/02
Andrew Geoffrey Milner	04/23/08
Richard L. Moore	01/01/98
Michael James Moran	12/19/07
John D. Morroco	05/07/69
Michael Patrick Murray	08/11/06
Gregory B. Norigian	01/01/98
Zaven R. Norigian	11/20/96
Aidan Kahlil Norton	04/27/05
Ryan Orsini	08/12/05
William A. Orsini, Jr.	03/16/05
Christopher Paolella	03/26/97
Aaron David Paolino	12/18/97
Andrew Carl Papino	08/12/05
Matthew Joseph Papino	01/01/99
Marc A. Pasquazzi	11/30/05
Alexander Justin Priest	08/12/08
Luca Antonio Fedeli Rebussini	09/16/10
Bryan J. Rekrut	11/12/95
Christopher Ryan Riccio	01/01/92
Matthew Blais Robillard	01/22/03

Joshua Read Robinson	10/17/07
Scott J. Salisbury	09/02/80
Michael Everett Sammartino	08/15/07
John Sandberg	09/12/64
Richard A. Sandberg	04/04/64
Mark F. Scott	01/31/70
Neil Scott	11/03/72
Richard H. Sharpe	05/02/68
Robert Michael Spinella	04/11/01
Michael P. Strayer	11/30/05
Kevin Paul Sturtevant	05/24/06
Harry F. Sunderland, Jr.	04/02/69
Augustus Tagliaferri	08/14/51
William Joseph Tirocchi III	05/24/06
Craig S. Turgeon	12/17/97
Nathan Ryan Umbriano	02/26/09
James M. Vartanian	06/06/79
Joseph Patrick Venagro	04/25/01
Barrett Michael Wall	03/12/08
John Charles Whipple, Jr.	03/14/07
Mark A. Williams	03/01/88
Thomas Francis Winemiller	12/03/09
Richard A. Zawislak, Jr.	01/15/91

PACK 8 TIVERTON

Sponsored by St. Christopher's Roman Catholic Church, 1660 Main Road, Tiverton, RI Pack 8 Tiverton was issued its first charter on September 19, 2007. The founder members are District Commissioner Jack Staskiewicz and Committee Chair Susan Miguel. The fledgling pack is off to a wonderful start and the boys are offered a diverse and ample program schedule.

Cubmasters for the Pack:

Mark Simoes 2008-present
Dan Pinckney 2008
Steve Desrosiers 2007

TROOP 10 PROVIDENCE

Troop 10 Providence is an ancient South Providence troop with a storied heritage of Scouting accomplishment. Initially gathered and organized in 1919, through the years it has evolved and progressed with the times, continuing to effectively serve the youth of an ever-changing community.

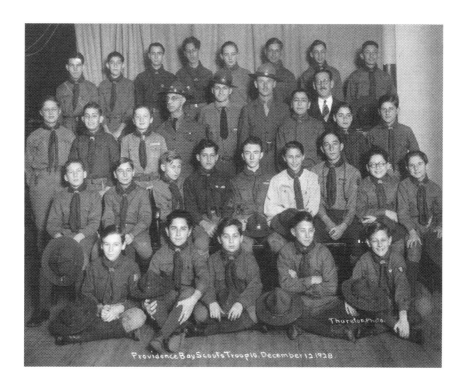

Troop 10 began almost entirely composed of young men of the Jewish Faith. Because of this we are fortunate to have an excellent account of Troop 10's early activities in an article entitled, "Jews and the Boy Scout Movement in Rhode Island" written by Eleanor F. Horvitz for the Rhode Island Jewish Historical Association. The brief history you are now reading draws heavily on Ms. Horvitz's research, and interested readers are encouraged to explore the entire original article.

Aaron Roitman, a Scout of Troop 10 and later a revered and respected leader of Narragansett Council, provided a great summary of the mission and success of Troop 10 in the years to follow. While the troop first continued to focus on Scouts of the Jewish faith, as the years went by it expanded its mission to serving youth from a variety of backgrounds:

"Here we were living in the toughest part of South Providence, children of immigrants, and we landed at scouting camp . . . We began to feel we were part of the whole community . . . we have to take the kids when they are young enough and integrate them into this society. Scouting is its own melting pot."

146

Aaron Roitman of Troop 10 Providence (1909 to 1995)

Troop 10 Providence was first chartered (1919 until 1923) to the Young Men's Hebrew Association, and the troop met at the Peace Street School. From 1924 until 1932 the chartering organization was the conservative Temple Beth Israel at 155 Niagara Street, which became the troop's meeting place for many years.

In the 1960's, Rabbi Harry Lasker (left), national Boy Scout director of Jewish relationships, and Rabbi Jacob Handler of Temple Beth Israel, confer Ner Tamid awards for exploration of the Jewish faith on Alan Goldberg (second from left) and Howard Goodman of Troop 10 Providence.

From 1923 until 1941 the building that housed the Temple and that was used by Troop 10 for its meetings was a structure that had originally been a German beer hall. In 1941 a brand new Temple was built at the same location, which, of course, improved the Scouting arrangement as well.

Beginning in 1933 the troop was chartered to the Jewish Veterans of Foreign Wars, Post No. 23, which continued to provide support until 1942. At that time the Men's Club of Temple Beth Israel assumed the chartering role, which they effectively fulfilled until the late 1970's.

Cub Scout from affiliated Cub Scout Pack 10 Providence learns more about Scouting at a 1952 Indian Pow Wow.

Reacting to continuing change in the community, the Calvary Baptist Church at 747 Broad Street became the chartering partner in the 1980's. An exception was 1984 when the troop was chartered to the Elmwood Community Center, the agency that now occupies the building at 155 Niagara Street originally built for Temple Beth Israel.

In the 1990's a final change took place when the chartering function was shifted from Calvary Baptist Church to the South Providence Neighborhood Ministries (SPNM), a non-denominational community agency that operates from the basement of Calvary Baptist Church. We are pleased to continue to celebrate the warm and supportive relationship that exists between Troop 10 Providence and SPNM.

Troop 10 under the adult leadership of Eagle Scout and Scoutmaster Kevin Kazlauskas conquers a New Hampshire mountain in 2005.

The following people have served as Scoutmaster through the years:

1919 to 1921	Maurice Goldsmith
1922	Philip H. Davison
1922	Bradford H. Field
1923 to 1929	Herman S. Galkin
1930 to 1932	Milton Fine
1933 to 1934	Oscar A. Leach
1935	Nathan Hodosh
1936	Saul Hodosh
1937 to 1939	Saul Pliner
1940	Irving Cohn
1941	Jerome Lamchick
1941	Mortimer Lamchick
1942	Irving Cohn
1943 to 1945	David Yanover
1946 to 1947	Mortimer I. Blender
1948 to 1949	Saul Hodosh
1950 to 1952	Stanley F. Turco (Troops 10 & 50)
1953 to 1958	Charles A. Strauss
1959 to 1960	Gerald A. Feldman
1961 to 1970	Louis J. Massover
1971 to 1972	Murray H. Massover
1973 to 1974	Lewis S. Sklaroff

1974	Richard Ballou
1974 to 1975	Louis J. Massover
1975	John J. Reis
1976 to 1980	Louis J. Massover
1981 to 1982	Gerald Fernandez
1982	Rolando Torres
1983	Angel A. Vega
1983	Gerald Fernandez
1984	Everett M. Gomes, Jr.
Late 1980's	John D. Baez
Early 1990's	Rolando Torres
1996	Wveimar Zapata
1997-1998	Victor A. Ross, Sr.
1999	Amy Blomires
2001	Amy L. Lomastro
2002 to 2004	Amy Lynn Snyder
2004	Brook Williams Weisman Ross
2005 to 2008	Kevin Antaya Kazlauskas
2009 to 2011	Jacob Foster Heimark

In addition to the leaders listed on Council records for the early 1920's, Ms. Horvitz speaks of a major leadership role played by Alfred Torgan (1921-22), Abraham Woodoff (1922), Harry Seltzer (1922), Alfred Geffner (1924-25), and Harold C. Sydney (1925).

Troop 10 under the leadership of Eagle Scout and Scoutmaster Brook Ross visits the Rhode Island Supreme Court in 2004, hosted by Distinguished Eagle Scout and Chief Justice Frank J. Williams.

The following have served as Chair of the Troop Committee:

1919 to 1921	Sidney Kapland
1922	Samuel Newburger
1923	Harry R. Rosen
1924	Benjamin N. Kane
1925	Barnet Roitman
1926	Albert C. Berger, DMD
1927	Arthur Gallatin
1928	Joseph Schlossberg
1929	Dr. Charles Hoffman
1930 to 1933	Dr. Carl Jagolinzer
1934	Dr. John J. Rouslin
1935	Irving D. Paster
1936 to 1937	Nathan Hodosh
1938	Irving Cohn
1939	Max A. Cohen
1940	Aaron Cohen
1941	Irving Cohn
1942	Saul Faber
1943 to 1945	Alton A. Gilstein
1946 to 1949	David Yanover
1950	N. Russell Swartz
1951 to 1952	Charles A. Strauss
1953 to 1954	Louis S. Bloom
1955	Bernard Cohen
1956	Barney Cohen
1957	Morris Press
1958	Jacob G. Wolff
1959 to 1963	Charles Goodman
1964	Charles Goodman
1965	David Morse
1966 to 1968	Achille R. Bessette
1969	Peter K. Rosedale
1970	Harvey Blake
1971 to 1975	Fred Kelman
1976 to 1980	Robert Johnson, Jr.
1981	Louis J. Massover
1982	Norma Luciano
1983 to 1995	Grace M. Wilcox
1996 to 1997	Norman D. Morris

1998	Victoria D. Thompson
1999 to 2002	Wanda Michaelson
2003 to 2005	Andrew M. Erickson
2006	James R. Essex
2007	Andrew M. Erickson
2008	James R. Essex
2009	Andrew M. Erickson
2010	James R. Essex
2011	Neil Ross

Current Troop Committee Chair Neil Ross (left) assisted by Assistant Scoutmaster John Togba Wright leads a trip to the United Nations for Troop 10 Providence and Troop 1 Kingston in 2005.

The following Troop 10 Providence Scouts have attained the rank of Eagle Scout:

Benton H. Rosen	08/27/29
Saul Friedman	04/21/30
Earle Cohn	08/24/39
Mortimer Lamchick	08/24/39
Roland Salk	12/19/42
Michael Greenspan	11/30/46
Albert Katz	04/12/47
Philip M. Shore	12/30/58
Irwin Chaiken	07/30/59
Horace G. Hamor, Jr.	08/13/61

| John Kilman | 03/22/73 | Allan Webster | 11/08/73 |

A number of noteworthy achievements by this "active, spirited troop" are described by Ms. Horvitz in the previously mentioned article. Troop 10 organized an orchestra, had its own newspaper, and also fielded a baseball team. Aaron Roitman reported that "Our troop always marched in the Memorial Day parades, and when the various scout troops met in Roger Williams Park for Field Day, we were proud of our winning record in all categories—scouting skills, starting a fire, and competitive games. We had a very active, very enthusiastic group. "

Mr. Roitman said, "Troop 10 was so popular. Kids will always go where the best action is. We had boys come all across the city to join our troop . . . We were very proud of that troop. We thought it was the greatest troop that ever existed."

Albert Katz of Troop 10 Providence (right), at his Eagle Scout Award Presentation conducted by Scout Commissioner O'Connell April 21, 1947.

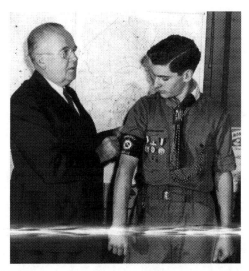

At the NC Annual Meeting January 8, 1942, Col. Webster, Chief of local Civilian Defense during World War II, recognizes Arnold Rose of Troop 10 for his Emergency Service.

A number of Troop 10 people have served with distinction at the Narragansett Council level. One person in particular must be considered in a class of his own. At age 80, Herman S. Galkin, Scoutmaster of Troop 10 from 1923 to 1929, was honored in 1977 by Eagle Scout and Governor J. Joseph Garrahy, who made March 18th Herman S. Galkin Day by special proclamation. Mr. Galkin received the prestigious Shofar Award on the same day.

Herman S. Galkin (1897 to 1980)

To recognize Herman S. Galkin for his service as a Scout since 1910 and a Scouter through his entire adult life, in 1982 his family donated the handicapped accessible Galkin Cabin, located to the right of the Bucklin Memorial Building and next to the Four Eagles Cabin. Herman S. Galkin's promotion of Scouting for boys of the Jewish faith and for the handicapped was truly exceptional. As another token of respect for his legacy, the Galkin Trail at Camp Yawgoog was named for him as well. Troop 10 is proud of the accomplishments of its former Scoutmaster.

One of the great recent strengths of Troop 10 has been a partnership arrangement with suburban troops. In particular, Troop 2 East Greenwich and its longstanding Scoutmaster Jim Essex (1965 to the present), have broadened considerably the array of available Scouting opportunities for Troop 10 Scouts. As Past Chair of the Troop 10 Troop Committee, Jim has time after time offered successful joint program options to both units. From sharing campsites at Camp Yawgoog, to marching together in parades, to joint flagging of the Veteran's Cemetery at Memorial Day, this has proven of great benefit to Scouts of both troops.

Under the adult leadership of Scoutmaster Amy Snyder, Troop 10 visits past Troop 2 East Greenwich Yawgoog Camper and Governor of the State of Rhode Island Don Carcieri in 2003.

Scouts of Troop 10 South Providence join with Scouts of Troop 2 East Greenwich in Flagging the Veteran's Cemetery in 2002

Another enriching experience for Troop 10 was conceived by Assistant Scoutmaster John Togba Wright, a recent immigrant to the United States fand now a naturalized American Citizen. As a former Scoutmaster in Liberia, John was keenly aware of the negative impact of the long civil war in his native country and the need to rebuild Scouting there from the ground up. John convinced the Troop Committee of Troop 10 to take a leadership role, which led to creation of the Bomamen Project (Bomamen means Good Turn in one of the Liberian tribal languages). New patches were designed and sent with stripped BSA uniforms and other supplies.

**Eagle Scout Evan Keith of Troop 1
Kingston collected over 100 uniforms to
send to Liberia with the new patches as
part of his Eagle Project.**

**John Togba Wright with one of the
shipments of Scouting Relief supplies
destined for Liberia**

The effort to help Liberian Scouts on their road to recovery is well on the way. Additional equipment has been sent, including funds for a computer and ten bicycles to be used by the Professional Staff of the Scouts of Liberia. John Togba Wright recently made available to Liberian Scouting a large tract of land outside Monrovia for vocational education and camping. New avenues of assistance are also being explored.

**The banner of Troop 10 Providence still proudly waves at Camp
Yawgoog's Dress Parade. Eagle Scout and present Scoutmaster
Jacob Foster Heimark, Senior Patrol Leader Marcus Ballard (right),
and Starlyn Nunez (left) lead the way.**

TROOP 13 PROVIDENCE

The story of Troop 13 Providence begins about a decade after the introduction of Scouting in Rhode Island when the Troop was organized and formally chartered in 1921. The Branch Avenue Neighborhood Center on the north side of downtown Providence sponsored the Troop. Meetings were held on Friday evenings in the gymnasium of the Esek Hopkins School, located at 480 Charles Street. Although the Troop stopped using the school as a meeting place in the early 1940s, the building still is active as a middle school in the Providence School System.

The Troop's first Scoutmaster was Herbert H. Boden, Sr. (1892-1960) who was born and raised in Boston, Massachusetts, and graduated from Mechanic Arts High School in 1910. The next three years he attended Evening Polytechnic School (a division of what would later become Northeastern University) while working as a licensed contractor and builder in Boston from 1912 to 1915 until he moved to Warwick, RI where he bought a small farm in the Hoxsie section of the city. He entered the teaching profession the following year and served as supervisor of manual arts and drawing in Bristol and Central Falls until December of 1917 when he enlisted in the U. S Army Signal Corps (Air Service) and saw overseas service in France during World War I with the 624nd Aero Squadron as a Corporal in the 42nd Balloon Company.

Upon his discharge in May of 1919 he was hired as an Instructor of Manual Arts in the Providence Public School System. In November of 1923 he became principal of Killingly Street disciplinary school and shortly thereafter supervising principal with assignments in most of the city's elementary schools until the time of his retirement in June of 1956. During these same years he received a Bachelor of Education degree from RI College of Education and did graduate work at Brown University and Providence College. He also served as a supervisor and assistant director of the Providence Junior Achievement Clubs for a number of years.

Herb first became associated with the boys of the North End in 1920. In May of that year Erik Anderson, then principal of the Providence Trade School, asked him if he would consider a project that would help to get some boys off the street and into a worthwhile activity. Accepting the proposal he gathered a group of boys to meet in the Old Greeley Street School basement one night a week under the sponsorship of the Branch Avenue Neighborhood Center. In September of 1920 the group moved to the Esek Hopkins School where they made tin-can toys and good use of the boys' gymnasium. It was just a short time later that a visit by Chief Scout Executive J. Harold Williams and Mr. Erik Jackson suggested the idea of converting the group into a Boy Scout troop. Convinced that it was the right thing to do and after checking with "his boys," he applied for a troop charter on March 24, 1921. Troop 13 was registered on May 30th with Herb as scoutmaster.

In several of the summers from 1921 to 1926 Herb was on the staff at Camp Yawgoog and records indicate that he served as camp Quartermaster. Chief Scout Executive, J. Harold Williams, recalls in *The Yawgoog Story: A Half Century of Scout Camping in Rhode Island, Vol I* (1965, p10.) a less serious side: But the gala event of the season was the annual appearance of "Barum and Bayrum's Circus." The grand march started down at the shore and ended at the "Opry House" where the audience assembled around the circus ring in front of the big open doors. Inside were the property rooms and staging areas. How well we remember Herb Boden and Gus Anthony as Ringmasters with their red military coats kepis and long cavalry swords, "Gus" on his motorcycle (before Model T Ford days), Ken Scott, the clown waiter, balancing a pile of dishes and a pitcher and finally soaking the Clown dinner-guest Cap Gunderson, Chief teetering back and forth on top of three tables, the Gilbane brothers doing the acrobatics, Goulding with his juggling, Fisher with his trained "animals".

Herb Boden led Troop 13 as Scoutmaster from 1921 until 1942 and remained on Troop Committee until 1959, even after moving to St. Petersburg, Florida for health reasons in 1956. For several years he served as Troop Committee Chairman. Herb was married to Marie J. Mathisen in June of 1921 and they raised two sons, one of whom attained the rank of Eagle Scout.

When Troop 13 was established, several other men in the community stepped up to help. Anthony Fraioli, Anthony Iuliano, Rocco Marcaccio, and Vincent Duva served as Assistant Scoutmasters. The initial Troop Committee consisted of the Chairman, Jesse H. Metcalf, Vincent Marcaccio, Henry Orabone, Anthony Coletti, and Dr. Genario R. Zinno. Senator Metcalfe (1860-1942) was a Providence businessman engaged in textile manufacturing and a philanthropist who had been a member of the RI House of Representatives and later became a US Senator from 1924-1937. He was involved in many civic activities including the Providence Common Council, chairman of the Metropolitan Park Commission of Rhode Island, a member of the penal and charitable board, president of Rhode Island Hospital, a trustee of the Rhode Island School of Design and of Brown University, and a Republican National Committeeman. He and his family were great benefactors of Camp Yawgoog and the Metcalfe Lodge in the Sandy Beach Division was dedicated in his honor in 1939. The Metcalfs owned the Wanskuck textile mill on Branch Avenue and thought that this new troop would be good for the development and character of the sons of the mill workers. It is recalled that the Metcalf family would provide a uniform for any boy that wanted to join the troop. Sometime in 1943, sponsorship of the Troop changed to the nearby Providence Boys' Club and meetings were held at the Wanskuck Club House located just a few streets away at 550 Branch Avenue. Hugh J. Smith took over temporarily as Scoutmaster. A year later Hugo M. Sanita became Scoutmaster and served at least until 1960. Hugo was 37 years old when he assumed leadership and had been involved with Scouting for 24 years.

The Providence Boys and Girls Club—Wanskuck Clubhouse today. Almost all Scouts in the early years were of Italian heritage. The following chart shows the number of boys officially registered as Scouts in the Troop as of the May re-registration date up to 1944, the last year of available data. Through the first decade membership grew steadily, even though a number of the boys were unable to afford uniforms.

Records indicate that there was some turn-over in the early years as boys moved away or lost interest. However, Troop activities—particularly hiking and over-night camping, Jamborees, parades, field days, rallies, archery club for the older boys, and participation in the North District Baseball League—kept boys in the Troop and attracted more every year until the Depression years when numbers fell back. Scouting was more than entertainment as the boys participated in "Good Turns" of the Council and District, prepared Thanksgiving and Christmas baskets for poor families in the neighborhood every year, and helped with church work and aid at cemeteries on Memorial Day. Chief Williams writes in *The Yawgoog Story* that the devastating fire of May 1930 left "our beautiful woods, except for about 50 acres, [a] black ruin. Our buildings were saved. We began at once to think of reforestation and how we could operate that summer." In response to that disaster Troop 13 sent two teams to help with reforestation in 1932 and also maintained a fire warning station for four weeks. At first, as in any new troop, most of the boys held the rank of Tenderfoot, but by 1928 some were earning merit badges.

By the end of the 1930s enrollments again climbed to about 30 Scouts every year. One of those Scouts was Michael Marra who later became a contractor and diesel engine mechanic and for a time served as a troop leader. Upon the retirement in 1956 of his Scoutmaster, Herb Boden, and to honor the influence on his life, Marra filled and graded a section along Camp Yawgoog Road to serve as a parking area for the vehicles of camping troops (original and replacement signs are shown below). The land also was used occasionally as an archery range and sports field in the 1960s.

Troop 13 continued actively through the fifties and sixties although not much information from this period has been found. Consequently it is unclear how long after 1960 Hugo M. Sanita served as Scoutmaster, but he continued to attend troop meetings for many years and remained an active participant. The following photo shows him instructing scouts on a camping trip at Buck Hill in 1979.

At some point he was succeeded by Pasco (Pat) Iuliano, the son of Anthony Iuliano who was one of the founding Troop Committee members. Pat Iuliano had been a scout in Troop 13 himself and grew up to become a photographer and music teacher at the Windmill Street Elementary School in Providence. He served as

Scoutmaster until 1983 with the help of Assistant Scoutmasters Paul Imbruglia, Phil Ianetta, and Larry Donahue.

In the later part of the 1970s the troop held numerous campouts at the various Narragansett Council properties—Aquapaug in South Kingstown, Champlin Reservation in Cranston, and Kelgrant in North Kingstown—as well as the Boys Club Camp Davis in Charlestown. The scouts also made special trips to Washington, DC in 1976, Philadelphia and Newport in 1977, Boston in 1978, and Fort Dix, NJ, in 1979. For a time, the Troop even had its own bus to transport boys and equipment.

From 1983 to 1989 Troop leadership was assumed by another of its former Scouts from the 1970s, Michael Piacente, who increased membership from a small number of boys up to a peak of forty-four. The Scouts participated in camporees, canoe trips, as well as regular scouting activities and camping at Yawgoog, Buck Hill in Burrillville, and The Boys' Club Camp Davis in Charlestown. Mike earned his Wood Badge—a program for adults that emphasizes leadership skills balanced by both Scoutcraft and program activities—during this time. Troop 13 also was served by Assistant Scoutmasters Michael Ianetta (son of former ASM Phil Ianetta) and John Currier. During this time the Troop moved its meeting place a short distance away from the Wanskuck Club House to the St. Ann's Church rectory on Greeley Street.

In 1990 the Troop was not re-chartered when Michael Piacente was unable to continue as Scoutmaster. This brought to a close a sixty-eight year history of Scouting in the Charles Street neighborhood in the North End of Providence. Through a succession of Scoutmasters, three of whom had been Scouts themselves, the Troop provided guidance, friendship, and fun for hundreds of boys. But the story of Troop 13 is about to add another chapter. After a twenty-year hiatus, steps are being taken to recharter the Troop 13 in 2010 and to resume its tradition of bringing the ideals of Scouting to boys living in the North End.

The Orabone family has had a long association with Troop 13, going back to troop committeeman, Henry Orabone. His son, Dick, was a member from 1952 through 1955 and recalls camping trips in Cranston and Warwick.

"Another of my camping trips was to Champlin Reservation on Scituate Avenue not far from my house. I remember we boarded the public bus (Union Transportation Company) on Phoenix Avenue to return home. The bus stop was right down the street from my home (all I had to do was turn around and see the property). Of course, my house wasn't built at that time because some of this area was still orchards and farming area." Henry's grandson Shawn Donahue recalls being in the Troop in the 1970s when Pasco Iuliano was the Scout Master, "Pasco made sure that we always had a local camp out at least once a month. We would go to Aquapaug, Davis, Buxton, Buck Hill, Skeleton Valley (Champlin), and of course Yawgoog. The troop grew to 70+ kids at the height and we had amazing annual bus trips to Washington DC, Gettysburg and Philadelphia. I ended up sticking with scouting and was fortunate to make Eagle Scout in the troop Grandpa helped to establish. Being on the Camp Yawgoog staff was a big highlight for me and I'm still in contact with many of the guys that were on staff with me back then."

Shawn also tells a story about his grandfather in the 1920s. ". . . our Great Grandmother was very upset and crying when she saw grandpa heading off to Camp Yawgoog the first time. Because of the uniform she was convinced he had been drafted and was going off to war! When he spent time at Yawgoog there was nothing but the Bucklin Building and the reservation trading post, which was their dining hall back then."

Eagle Scouts from Troop 13 Providence

Albert Alianiello	02/10/31
Shawn R. Donahue	05/13/81
Bryan J. Gordon	06/10/84
Robert Hearne	08/14/51
Pasco Iuliano	04/05/37
Pasco S. Iuliano	08/20/64
Michael Marra	08/18/49
Henry Orabone, Jr.	08/30/45
Joseph Pignatelli	12/29/28

TROOP 15 CHARLESTOWN

Date of original charter: 04/30/75
Chartering organization and dates: Church of the Holy Spirit 1975-current
Scoutmasters and dates of service if known

Name	Date served	Date ended
Harold Bethel	4/75	4/76
William Grove	4/76	4/77
David Cesaro	4/77	4/80
David Greene	4/80	4/81
Albert Kellers Sr.	4/81	4/90
William Follett Sr.	4/90	3/03
Phillip Lee	3/03	6/09
Frank Thoman	6/09	-

Number of Eagle Scouts

As of 11/22/2008 Troop 15, Charlestown has produced 47 Eagle Scouts

Andrew Robert Andre	02/27/03
Jiray Gregory Avedisian	12/28/09
Mark Addison Baker	03/03/10
Nicholas John Bilotta	07/15/02
Connor Wedesweiler Capizzano	08/23/06
Anthony J. Ciringione	04/14/04
Christopher Robert Clarkin	09/15/10
Andrew Newton Deslaurier	12/14/93
Justin Ronald Enos	11/10/05
Ronald Armando Fasano	11/10/05
Vincent Albert Fasano	02/20/06
Andrew Charles Follett	11/15/05
Christopher J. C. Follett	12/01/87
Steven P. Follett, Jr.	12/16/97
William E. Follett, Jr.	10/30/82
Gary Michael Fullerton	01/30/91
Kyle Daniel Gardiner	11/20/10
Andrew David Gardner	04/12/00
Peter Nathaniel Gardner	03/07/02
Andrew R. Girard	10/23/04
Robert Greene, Jr.	04/25/86
Richard F. Heines	10/05/85
Arthur K. Howe, Jr.	04/11/91
Albert C. Keller, Jr.	06/22/83
Keith Michael Kennedy	01/13/07
Wesley R. Laurent	09/05/91
Casey P. Lee	05/20/03
Christopher Patrick Lee	05/24/06
Christopher Thomas Louzon	03/19/08
Stephen Craig Louzon	03/24/04
Jonathan W. Lyons	01/01/99
John K. MacCoy, Jr.	01/01/94
Sean S. McIntire	03/18/93
Christopher Pater	12/01/04
John H. Poirier	07/11/88
Bryan Patrick Poston	11/22/08
Thor Rutger Quimby	08/07/07
Patrick Brendan Quirk	11/20/10

Brian Wayne Rhodes	03/18/93
Jesse W. Rhodes	07/29/95
Ryan Joseph Rhodes	01/01/98
Scott Richardson	12/09/88
Jason Raymond Ringler	10/05/90
Travis W. Ringler	07/03/97
Daniel M. Rzewuski	06/06/89
Michael R. Schipritt	06/16/93
Thomas Anthony Schipritt	01/01/99
Andrew T. Schneider	06/16/04
William C. Towne, Jr.	04/06/84
Christopher Evans Turgeon	01/13/07
Robert Allison Walsh	10/03/07
Kevin J. Whaley	08/07/87

Notable Alumni
Jason Ringler earned the Hornaday bronze medal
Andrew Gardner, graduated West Point Academy

Additional items of interest, camp history, war service, unique events, etc.

We were considered the rain troop for the first four years because every time we camped it rained.

Yawgoog—originally camped at (SB or MB) then moved to Camp Three Point—campsite Zucculo

Unit Chronology: a brief history of your unit highlighting key points in your unit history.

West Point 2002, 2008, 2009
Adult Leader landed a helicopter in the fields of Gardner Farms 2008

TROOP 15 FALL RIVER

The first charter for Troop 15 Fall River was issued on March 1, 1937. The unit has always been sponsored by Notre Dame De Lourdes Roman Catholic Church located at 529 Eastern Avenue, Fall River, MA. At that time, the troop met at Notre Dame School. In the 1990's the meeting location changed to the church hall. From late 2004-2008, the troop held its meetings at the Union United Methodist Church on Highland Avenue in Fall River and held a "duel" sponsorship with the church. The unit now meets in the Notre Dame Parish Hall beside the church.

The Scoutmasters of Troop 15 Fall River

Timothy Beaulieu	2009-present
David Craig Deston	2009
Frederick P. Ramsay, III	2008-2009
Jose A. DaMota, Jr	2004-2007
Joseph A. Primo	
Paul A. Dumais, Jr	1984-
Leo R. Boutin	1980-1884
Richard K. Cloutier	1979-1980
Claude Gelinas	1976-1979
William P. Bouchard	1976 (died on 9/25/76 at the age of 49)

The Eagle Scouts of Troop 15 Fall River

Cory Leonardo	09/24/2008	Jonathan Ferry	07/29/1998
Alexander H. Sheehan	05/16/2007	Matthew Soares	06/17/1998
Stafford W. Sheehan	12/13/2006	Kevin Donovan	10/01/1997
Tyler R. Hill	11/12/2006	Paul Ferland	05/14/1997
Brendan Scott McNerney	07/05/2006	Daniel Lussier, II	06/29/1996
Timothy Nicoletti	01/12/2005	John Bronhard, II	09/15/1993
Mitchell Coughlin	06/04/2003	David Deston, Jr.	06/17/1992
Robert M. Boutin	10/09/2002	Rodney Thibault	06/05/1991
Michael Gilles Canuel	07/25/2001	Omer Thibault, III	10/15/1989
Timothy Morton	07/19/2000	Gregory Primo	06/14/1989
Matthew Coughlin	05/17/2000		
Christopher Dionne	10/14/1998		

TROOP 18 CRANSTON (1934-1978)

Troop 18 Cranston met at Daniel D. Waterman Elementary School on Pontiac Avenue in Cranston for its entire 44 year existence.

In its prime, Troop 18 was truly a powerhouse, well known throughout Narragansett Council as one of only two troops using the classic Campaign Hats and white gloves as part of their Class A uniforms for troop meetings, parades and other special occasions.

**Bob Rachlow keeps Troop 18 in step as they march
in the 1954 Cranston Bicentennial Parade**

It was originally chartered on December 20, 1934, to a "Group of Citizens", and retained strong community support until new circumstances led to discontinuation of unit operations January 31, 1978.

Founded in the midst of the Great Depression, Troop 18 focused on building responsible citizenship on the part of its members. A letter to Chief Williams dated March 26, 1937 from Scoutmaster Stanley Bamforth concerned repayment of nine dollars for a broken window at Camp Yawgoog and read as follows:

"The three boys who participated in the window breaking episode have to pay the damages from their own pocket, as is only logical, but seeing that one of the boys' parents are in rather poor financial condition at the present time, this boy is paying his share on the installment plan."

**Troop 18 Cranston in 1954 camping
at Doric Masonic Center on Reservoir Avenue**

A change in the troop chartering arrangement occurred on January 20, 1948, when the Kiwanis Club of Cranston became the Chartering Organization for the troop's final thirty years.

The following leaders served as Scoutmasters:

Stanley R. Bamforth	1934-1936
William R. Hartland	1937-1938
Nathan Barlow Swift	1939
Stanley R. Bamforth	1940-1942
Francis C. McCormick	1943-1946
John Pollitt	1947
Vincent Morvillo	1948
Malcolm L. Daniels	1949-1953
Robert V. Rachlow	1954-1957
Richard E. Vandall	1958-1959
Alden L. Redfern	1960
Malcolm L. Daniels	1961-1964
Warren Grogan, Jr.	1965-1968
Anthony G. Ruggieri	1969
Norman E. Richard	1970-1971
James E. Burdick, Sr.	1972
Richard Kizirian	1973-1978

In 1954 Troop 18 Cranston was considered one of the best equipped troops in Narragansett Council.

The following citizens served as Troop Committee Chairs:

William W. Noonan	1934-1935
Ragnar Swanson	1936-1939
Armand Lanoie	1940-1942
Hon. James L. Taft	1943-1947
Jack Greenberg	1948-1952
Michael A. Gelardi	1953-1956
John A. Fitzsimon	1957
Rolf Johnson	1958
Milton S. Pelosi	1959
Joseph Smith	1960-1964
Ralph Paola, Jr.	1965-1969
John F. Jones	1970-1971
Richard Kizirian	1972
Christian L. Kilguss	1973
Warren Grogan, Jr.	1974
William H. Rizzini	1975
Kenneth Cahoon	1976-1978

Each patrol had its own wall tent and cooking chest with a complete set of cooking utensils and supplies. The adult here is Scoutmaster Peppy Daniels.

Troop 18 Cranston had an extremely positive impact on the lives of hundreds of young men who grew through participation in the Scouting experience as troop members. Troop 18 graduates have distinguished themselves as outstanding citizens who have made a real difference in their lives and vocations.

Troop 18 retained and enhanced its reputation for organizational strength and good equipment in the 1960's and 1970's as camping styles changed and the troop grew to a total of 78 members.

The following Scouts attained the rank of Eagle Scout:

James Edward Hunter	1939	03/27/39
Fred T. Miner	1939	03/27/39
Oscar K. Swanson	1939	03/27/39
Robert Gershkoff	1940	04/08/40
Arthur W. Butler, Jr.	1942	05/23/42
James F. Felch	1944	08/24/44
Robert C. Felch	1945	08/30/45
Arthur Edwin Erickson, Jr.	1946	11/30/46
Andrew Martin Erickson	1954	08/15/54
Kenneth R. Wing	1955	08/30/55
Raymond Robert Culgin, Jr.	1956	08/04/56

John Leclair	1956	08/04/56
Hudson B. Scattergood	1956	08/04/56
Frank H. Wilbur	1960	03/01/60
Steven Ford	1966	10/05/66
Gary Scott Holt	1968	02/22/68
Sebastian S. Santoro	1968	02/22/68
Frank Donald McKendall	1968	05/02/68
Michael J. Jones	1968	10/29/68
Randy Lamchick	1969	05/07/69
Robert R. Lombari	1969	11/15/69
James M. Grogan	1970	05/13/70
Michael I. Grant	1971	02/06/71

Troop 18 Scoutmaster Warren Grogan pins Eagle Badges on (L to R) new Eagle Scouts Don McKendall, Sebastian Santoro, and Gary Holt at the 1969 troop Annual Dinner.

The activities of Troop 18 were well chronicled in the 1950's by an award-winning newspaper, Highlights of Troop 18. The paper was created, written, and independently produced by the Scouts of the Flying Eagle Patrol, who sold it to other troop members for the princely sum of 5 Cents a copy.

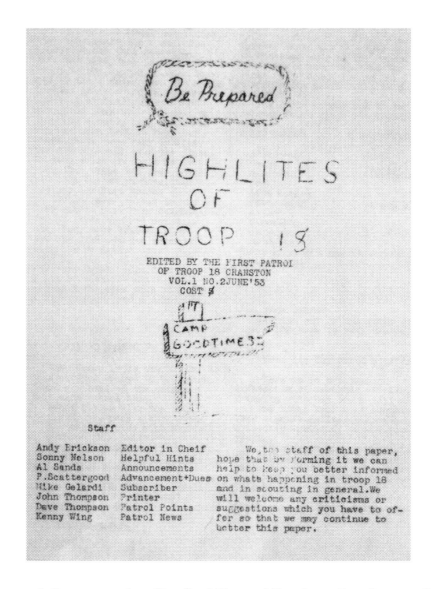

A few representative excerpts will reflect Troop 18's strengths. As was the norm in Scouting at the time, boy-led patrol events, usually without adult presence, formed the heart of Scouting in the troop.

A 1954 article headed "Vacation Hiking" follows:

The warden of Skeleton Valley, Roy Simmonds, stated that during the period of February 22-27 the number of hikers and campers was more abundant than at any other time he can remember.

There were several hikes held by the various patrols in our troop. The Bat Patrol held two camping trips. The first was 3 days and the second was two days. The Cobra Patrol held 3 day trips.

The Flying Eagle Patrol held one day trip. The Flaming Arrow Patrol held two trips. The first was an overnight trip, and the second was a day talk. The Pioneer Patrol held one overnight trip.

In the same issue the Patrol Yells were recorded. The Bat Patrol, for instance, used the following:

Although our patrol is not high hatty,
We will drive the others batty,
We have members brave and bold,
We hike in the warm, we hike in the cold.

**Troop 18 camping at Skeleton Valley (Champlain) on June 11, 1950.
Photo supplied by Eagle Scout Bob Culgin.**

Unabashed by the troop authority structure, an independent voice was maintained on the Editorial Page.

For example, in encouraging improvement in the program provided by leadership at troop meetings the Staff commented, "With pride comes neglect of duties, and in such a way our troop has gradually slipped."

It is a tribute to the adult troop leadership that no attempt was made to reign in the views of the Scouts. Later stories indicated that the Scouts' call to action was indeed heeded.

**Troop 18 on one of its many Canoe Camping trips
through the Great Swamp in the 1960's and 1970's.**

The following open Letter to Parents also reflects troop culture:

Dear Parents,

We would like to impress on you the great fun a Scout gets out of winter camping and the relatively few dangers incurred on such a hike. Don't get us wrong, though. There are many—without adequate leadership that is.

Of course YOU don't have to worry about that. Every Patrol Leader in OUR troop is an Explorer and well suited to take on such an extra amount of responsibility. We hope that you will urge on instead of hold back your son. Remember—the responsibilities you place in your son now will form a strong character and will greatly help him in the years to come.

Sincerely, THE STAFF

**Eagle Scout Jack Leclair demonstrates gourmet cooking
on a 1956 camping trip in New Hampshire.**

Encouragement from Chief Williams, based on his own background of writing as a reporter, was regular and enthusiastic. On one occasion the Highlights of Troop 18 received and published the following letter from the Chief, entitled "Meeting Baden-Powell".

The Scouts of Troop 18 Cranston and the readers of HIGHLITES may be interested in reading about my only meeting with Lord Robert Baden-Powell, the Chief Scout of the World.

It was the early 1920's in Boston. It was in late winter and the weather was cold and blustery. But the Chief Scout walked through the streets from his hotel to the meeting place in his Scout shorts.

He was a very genial and pleasant man, with a warm smile and a face covered with freckles and little lines from much outdoor life in the sun.

I remember distinctly one story he told. This is it.

"At a recent patrol leaders' conference in London, the question was asked, 'What do you do with a rotter, a bad boy, in the troop?'"

"One patrol leader stood up and said, "My father is a green grocer and when he finds a rotten apple in the apple barrell, he picks it out and chucks it away so that it will not spread the rot to the other apples. That's what we should do with a rotter in the troop. Throw him out!'

Then another Patrol Leader rose. He said, 'My father is a horse dealer. When he gets a bad horse, he doesn't shoot him. He harnesses him between two good horses and they pull him straight. So that's what we should do with a poor Scout. Get him working with two good scouts and they will straighten him out."

J. Harold Williams, SCOUT EXECUTIVE March 24, 1954

At a Council promotional event in 1956 to encourage religious awards, Pete Scattergood of Troop 18, on left, (later an Eagle Scout) represents Protestant Scouts who have received the God and Country Award, and Mike Gelardi of Troop 18, on right, represents Roman Catholic Scouts who have received the Ad Altare Dei Award.

A number of Troop 18 Scouts have served with distinction in the military, from World War II to Viet Nam. Some, like Malcolm "Peppy" Daniels, were wounded and carried with them imbedded shrapnel fragments for the rest of their lives. We are most fortunate that our returning veterans provided strong adult leadership to Scouting in Troop 18 and elsewhere.

During World War II, when many Scoutmaster-age adults were serving our country, Troop 18 was able to survive and prosper due to strong adult Troop Committees chaired by the likes of Judge James L. Taft, as well as strong youth leaders who rose to the challenge and demonstrated the Scouting ideal of boys leading boys.

Regular Troop 18 summer camping at Camp Yawgoog traditionally used the Oak Ridge Campsites in Three Point. Annual participation in District camping at Mount Monadnock was extremely popular. One year the Monadnock experience was particularly memorable when Scoutmaster Peppy Daniels broke his war-weakened leg during the ascent, requiring emergency rescue.

Led by Senior Patrol Leader Jack Leclair (left kneeling) and adult supervision under Scoutmaster Bob Rachlow (right), the Explorers of Troop 18 head north in 1955 for some serious camping and hiking.

Of Troop 18's many notable alumni, one in particular has continued and enhanced the heritage and some of the traditions of Troop 18 Cranston. The 18th Eagle Scout of Troop 18, Don McKendall, was the founding Scoutmaster of Troop 5 North Kingstown, chartered to the Rotary Club of North Kingstown.

Troop 5 became a stellar troop, one that has delivered Scouting to its members with distinction and class. Other Troop 18 graduates salute the accomplishments of Troop 5 and Don McKendall as exemplars of much that once made Troop 18 an excellent troop.

TROOP 20 CRANSTON

Unit & community: Troop 20 Cranston, Rhode Island
Year chartered: 1951
Chartering organization: Eden Park Elementary School Parent Teachers Association
Meeting location: Old Eden Park Fire Barn, corner of Branch & Colonial Avenues
First Troop Leaders on chartering
Scoutmaster: William Clough

Committee: Neil F. Ross (treasurer), Carlton Brown, Keith Lawrence, George Houth, Everett Brown *(partial list)*
Senior Patrol Leader: Earle Perkins
Assistant SPL: Roderick McGarry, II

TROOP HISTORY:

Troop 20 began with about 30 Scouts in four patrols. It first attended Camp Yawgoog in the summer of 1952 camping in Manchosi, beside the waterfront, in the Medicine Bow Division. It always participated in the Cranston District's annual Columbus Holiday weekend fall camporee at Mount Monadnock in New Hampshire.

During the year the troop and/or individual patrols would hike from the Fire Barn down Colonial Avenue and follow the Scituate Aqueduct to camp at Skeleton Valley Scout Camp (later renamed Champlin Reservation) at 223 Scituate Avenue in western Cranston. The troop often marched in the City of Cranston parades down Park Avenue including the big Bicentennial Celebration of 1954.

Troop 20 went inactive in the late 1970s and disbanded, with continuing Scouts transferring to Troop 7 Cranston that met at the Waterman Elementary School basement.

30 EAGLE SCOUTS

Scout	*Year Court of Honor*
Neale McGarry	1953 08/16/53
Roderick A. McGarry, II	1953 08/16/53
Richard Webster	1953 12/19/53
Norbert Fleisig	1954 12/18/54
John M. Geisser	1954 08/15/54
Raymond Arthur Briggs	1955 12/17/55
Howard Alan Bryne	1955 08/30/55
Geoffrey A. Clough	1955 12/17/55
John J. DeMizio, Jr.	1955 08/30/55
Ralph E. Carriolo	1956 08/04/56
George N. Houth, Jr.	1956 08/04/56
David C. Brown	1957 08/10/57
Kenneth N. Lawrence	1957 08/10/57
Edward A. Ramsey	1957 08/10/57
Richard R. Stone	1957 08/10/57
Anthony J. Ramsey	1958 12/13/58

Martin Smith	1959 07/30/59
Gordon C. Lawrence	1961 08/13/61
Robert W. Osterberg	1961 08/13/61
Gregory Ahlijian	1962 08/04/62
Mark R. Serdjenian	1965 05/22/65
Jeffrey N. Davis	1970 03/15/70
Paul J. Lockett	1970 10/31/70
Garnet W. Brown	1971 12/01/71
Carl R. Perry	1971 05/11/71
Lawrence W. Trahan	1971 12/01/71
Richard Horne	1972 12/12/72
Joseph DiPalma	1975 11/18/75
Donald C. Mattera	1975 12/29/75
James G. Dolan	1976 01/13/76

TROOP 21 SOMERSET

The Troop's first charter was issued on April 1st, 1945. It is currently sponsored by the Somerset Lion's Club.

Scoutmasters of Troop 21 from 1945-present

James Nichols	1945
Frank Osbaldeston	1950
Daniel Koohey	1951
Joseph Benevides	1952
Thomas Dolan	1953
Arthur Marsden	1958
John Souza 1962 (died while SM at the age of 42)	
Charles Rowe, Jr.	1964
David Lowney	1965
Frederick Hutchinson	1968
Robert Paine	1970
John Kinnane	1971
Thomas Paine	1972
Charles Targee	1973
Denis Auclair	
Michael Francoeur	1996
Jeffrey Messier	2005-

Eagle Scouts from Troop 21 Somerset

Fernand C. Auclair, Jr.	11/24/64
Matthew James Baker	06/09/10
Michael C. Berard	10/30/81
Nicholas Dennis Bernier	12/28/98
Robert Broughton	04/05/49
John Roger Charest	10/14/09
Andrew Ryan Correia	08/13/09
Shaun Michael Correia	08/13/09
Andrew Davis	12/20/04
Sheldon A. Davis	10/24/63
Michael E. DeMoranville	02/20/07
Timothy Robert DeMoranville	08/20/01
Larry Feilhauer	11/27/61
Donald Flores	11/03/60
Daniel P. Francoeur	11/09/05
Matthew D. Francoeur	03/07/02
Daniel M. Gamache	09/28/06
Maurice E. Hardy	11/22/64
William G. Heroux	11/24/64
Brendan J. Marden	08/23/10
Keith A. Marsden	11/03/60
Robert Joseph McGlynn	12/15/10
Brendan Michael Meehan	04/26/07
Brendan K. Mello	12/18/07
Jason K. Mello	12/12/02
Peter Menard	10/25/07
Marc Jerome Messier	10/09/08
Matthew Messier	12/15/10
Stephen Edward Murphy	12/15/10
Kieran P. Murray	08/23/10
Nicholas Anthony Nogueira	11/14/05
Andrew Lawrence Nunes	07/30/01
Edmond Nunes	03/13/28
Edmund M. Nunes	01/03/00
Kevin Scott O'Brien	09/16/08
Shayne P. Parent	11/20/03
Andrew David Patota	07/26/05
Daniel G. Proulx	08/21/74

Richard L. Pyatt	04/25/67
Robert S. Pyatt, Jr.	02/25/64
Benjamin A. Reed	12/28/98
Nicholas Alex Reed	03/07/02
Wayne N. Rousseau	02/06/86
Nathaniel C. Sheehan	10/22/03
Robert A. Souza	11/07/62
Chad Dana Stewart	07/26/05
Michael D. Sypko	10/24/63
William Travers	05/09/94
Robert William Umland	01/01/67
James M. Waring	11/03/60
Stephen M. Wilusz	09/26/67

TROOP 26 SWANSEA

Original charter date unknown, but the unit has been in existence for at least 55 years.

Chartering Organization: Up to 1975, Swan Finishing Company. Starting in 1975 Knights of Columbus, Swansea, MA.

Scoutmasters:

John Pysz			
Fred Mason	1967-68	John Greenwood	1992-94
Paul Parente	1978-85	Charley Pelissier	1994-98
Al Stiles	1979-86	Steve Woodruff	1998-03
Don Terry	1986-87	Charley Pelissier	2003-05
Charley Pelissier	1988-92	Ron Toland	2005-Present

Eagle Scouts: Since 1952-66 (see below)

Notable Alumni; Scouting; 3 Silver Beavers—Paul Parente, Al Stiles, Charley Pelissier

Items of Interest: Isaac Davis Trail
Maine National High Adventure Area
Scout Shows (former Moby Dick Council)
West Point weekends
Gettysburg National Park

Summer Camp every year
Monthly campouts during program year
Boston Freedom Trail
Antietam Battlefield

EAGLE SCOUTS from Troop 26 Swansea

Fernand C. Auclair, Jr.	11/24/64
Matthew James Baker	06/09/10
Michael C. Berard	10/30/81
Nicholas Dennis Bernier	12/28/98
Robert Broughton	04/05/49
John Roger Charest	10/14/09
Andrew Ryan Correia	08/13/09
Shaun Michael Correia	08/13/09
Andrew Davis	12/20/04
Sheldon A. Davis	10/24/63
Michael E. DeMoranville	02/20/07
Timothy Robert DeMoranville	08/20/01
Larry Feilhauer	11/27/61
Donald Flores	11/03/60
Daniel P. Francoeur	11/09/05
Matthew D. Francoeur	03/07/02
Daniel M. Gamache	09/28/06
Maurice E. Hardy	11/22/64
William G. Heroux	11/24/64
Brendan J. Marden	08/23/10
Keith A. Marsden	11/03/60
Robert Joseph McGlynn	12/15/10
Brendan Michael Meehan	04/26/07
Brendan K. Mello	12/18/07
Jason K. Mello	12/12/02
Peter Menard	10/25/07
Marc Jerome Messier	10/09/08
Matthew Messier	12/15/10
Stephen Edward Murphy	12/15/10
Kieran P. Murray	08/23/10
Nicholas Anthony Nogueira	11/14/05
Andrew Lawrence Nunes	07/30/01

Edmond Nunes	03/13/28
Edmund M. Nunes	01/03/00
Kevin Scott O'Brien	09/16/08
Shayne P. Parent	11/20/03
Andrew David Patota	07/26/05
Daniel G. Proulx	08/21/74
Richard L. Pyatt	04/25/67
Robert S. Pyatt, Jr.	02/25/64
Benjamin A. Reed	12/28/98
Nicholas Alex Reed	03/07/02
Wayne N. Rousseau	02/06/86
Nathaniel C. Sheehan	10/22/03
Robert A. Souza	11/07/62
Chad Dana Stewart	07/26/05
Michael D. Sypko	10/24/63
William Travers	05/09/94
Robert William Umland	01/01/67
James M. Waring	11/03/60
Stephen M. Wilusz	09/26/67

TROOP 39 SUMMIT

Unit & Community:	TROOP 39 SUMMIT, RI
Date of Original Charter:	MARCH 1964
Chartering Organization:	SUMMIT BAPTIST CHURCH
	1176 VICTORY HIGHWAY
	COVENTRY, RI 02816

Scoutmasters:	1.	George Skaling (d)	1964-68
	2.	Alfred Gaulien	1969
	3.	Thomas Greene	1970
	4.	Ed Ramsey	1971
	5.	George Morton	1972-75
	6.	Wayne Luther	1976-78
	7.	Mike Reposa	1979-80
	8.	Bob O'Neill (d)	1981
	9.	George Miller	1982-83
	10.	Bill Albro	1984-85
	11.	Ed Schultz	1986-87
	12.	Bernie George	1988-

Number of Eagle Scouts: 45

Notable Alumni:	Eagle #6:	DR. ERIC M. GEORGE, DMD
	Eagle #13:	CPT. J.PATRICK HUGHES, USAF
Items of Interest:		For 27 years, the troop has been doing Turkey Campouts. The largest number of people that have been fed is 241 (16 turkeys). Admission to the event is a donation for the Coventry Food Bank.
Unit Chronology:		Camp Yawgoog (44 YEARS)
		Allagash, ME—100 Mile Canoe Trip
		St. Croix, ME—100 Mile Canoe Trip
		Mount Katadin, ME—Razors Edge
		Century Bike Ride—100 Miles in one day
		N-S Trail (77.3) and 33 miles in Maine—100 Mile Hikes in one year
		Road Bikes 50 Miles to Yawgoog

Troop 39 Summit Eagle Scouts

Christopher W. Albro	04/09/90
Geoffray Curtis Albro	02/17/96
Patrick Robert Arrico	03/24/05
Steven Michael Autieri	01/01/99
Michael Arthur Bennett	12/23/08
Nicholas Paul Brown	01/01/99
Nicholas Michael Cinquegrana	12/06/10
Edward Nicholas Cole	04/13/09
William Henry Cole IV	03/18/07
Justin Robert Dugas	08/02/00
Eric Michael George	03/04/92
Todd M. George	06/28/85
Kevin Mark Gravier	12/02/05
Aaron C. Greene	09/18/91
Evan Mathew Hall	11/07/97
Ryan Michael Hall	01/01/99
Forest J. Handford	03/04/93
David K. Hankins	06/29/00
Nicholas Kevin Hankins	04/18/03

Kevin David Harrington	10/15/08
Andrew Robert Hevey	10/08/09
John Patrick Hughes	11/15/97
Derek Earl Jervis	01/23/01
Mark Jesse Jordan	01/06/02
Matthew Ryan Karwoski	06/29/00
Nicholas David Kettle	07/03/08
Erik James H. Kinsella	06/30/05
William Lagerstrom	02/13/74
Joshua Paul Lessard	12/06/10
Thomas Drury Lockwood	09/04/09
Douglas Marques	06/03/87
Edward Charles Morgan	12/27/96
Patrick Ryan Morgan	06/20/02
George M. Morton	02/13/74
Matthew Daniel Paquette	09/04/09
Michael J. Petrarca	11/11/91
Nathan W. Powers	08/27/03
Mark E. Randolph	05/05/94
Joseph Edward Scambio	07/12/00
William A. Sheldon	11/02/04
Daniel John Shields	05/22/09
Jeremy P. Skaling	03/15/95
Samuel Geoffrey Slezak	11/05/10
Tyler John Slezak	11/25/07
Justin Chafee Standish	07/16/04
Matthew MacGregor Stephenson	11/20/00
Eric James Toomey	03/18/07
Jason Michael Waldeck	11/05/06

TROOP 63 WESTPORT

- **Unit & Community**: Troop #63, Westport, MA

- **Date of Original Charter**: 1977

- **Chartering Organization(s) & Dates**:
  Westport Point United Methodist Church, 1977-Present

- **Scoutmasters/Cubmasters & Dates of Service (if known):**

Donn Levesque	1977-1981
Bruce Beaulieu	1981-1982
Ken Turner	1982-1986
Robert Roy	1986
Ken Turner	1987-3/1991
Donn Robidoux	3/1991-11/1997
John Gifford	11/1997-3/2008
Chris Brayton	3/2008-Present

Eagle Scouts from Troop 63 Westport

Jonathan A. Briggs	01/26/83
John H. Chambers	07/02/03
Ian Matthew Costanzo	06/29/10
Peter Desjardins	01/01/91
Andrew John Gifford	11/21/02
Seth Gifford	01/01/01
Peter William Holmstrom	07/26/01
Nicholas M. Kiefer	04/25/97
George A. Marceau, III	10/06/85
James Alden Mauck	05/02/02
Robert William McMillan	07/05/01
Raymond W. Morin	01/26/83
Keith E. Nickelson	09/03/92
Ryan S. Nickelson	11/09/95
Ryan Matthew Palmer	09/21/10
David Leonard Potter	10/12/97
Nolan A. Robidoux	08/30/94
Sean A. Robidoux	11/20/96
Kyle F. Tripp	04/29/99
Wayne H. Turner	09/17/85
Alan Walters	07/25/29
Alan T. Walters	01/07/99
Anthony E. Ward	08/03/95
Jonathan E. Ward	06/30/93

- **Notable Alumni**:
Jonathan A. Briggs, Raymond W. Morin, Wayne H. Turner, John F. Paddock, Peter Desjardins, Keith E. Nickelson, Jonathan E. Ward, Nolan A. Robidoux,

Anthony "Tony" Ward, Ryan S. Nickelson, Sean A. Robidoux, Nicholas M. Kiefer, David L. Potter, Alan T. Walters, Kyle F. Tripp, Seth T. Gifford, Robert W. McMillan, Peter W. Holmstrom, James A. Mauck, Andrew J. Gifford, John H. Chambers II

- **Additional Items of Interest: camp history, war service, unique events, etc.:** Attend Camp Cachalot annually, camp at Disneyworld's Fort Wilderness every 2 years +/-, for 20+ years have sold Christmas wreaths as an annual fundraiser

- **Unit Chronology: A brief history of your unit highlighting key points in your unit's history:** Philmont 1997, Philmont 1999, Sea Base 2008

PACK 164 ASSONET

While the history is incomplete for Cub Scout Pack 164 of Assonet, it is believed that the original Charter Organization was Algonquin Gas (it's on the Pack flag). At some point in time (presumably after the closing of the Algonquin Gas facility), charter of the pack was picked up by K.R.R. Inc. Operation of the Pack was taken over by Gary and Jeanne Vander Kaaden in 1992, who ran it until 2002. During this time, Pack 164, meeting at the United Church of Assonet, was very active, and with the involvement of a dedicated cadre of adult leaders the Pack participated in many of the activities that are familiar to anyone who has been a Cub Scout; sleepovers at the Museum of Science in Boston and on the Battleship Massachusetts, annual "Pinewood Derby" car races, and Halloween parties with the ever popular "donut races" to name just a few.

Having run the Pack for two years after their youngest son had "crossed over" into Boy Scout Troop 164, which he had founded; Mr. Vander Kaaden handed the reigns over to Desiree Logan, who kept it running for another year until the Logans no longer had any sons in Cub Scouts. Unfortunately, there was no one willing to assume the role of Cubmaster and the charter was allowed to lapse. Since that time, Peter Ashworth, former District Executive for the Massasoit District, Narragansett Council and Diane Cloutier, his successor, have worked to reestablish a Pack in Assonet. Pack 164 was rechartered by St. Bernard Catholic Church. On a historical note, Massasoit District (and Cachalot District, which Troop and Pack 64 of East Freetown are a part) were both part of Moby Dick Council, which merged with Narragansett Council. Both of those districts were at one time Councils (Cachalot Council was first known as New Bedford Council and Massasoit as Fall River Council). Moby Dick Council came into being c. 1971, and it merged with Narragansett Council in 2000.

TROOP 164 ASSONET

It has been said that there have been several Boy Scout Troops in Assonet over the years and that none lasted for very long. In an interview, Mr. Lynwood French recalled that the first Troop (Troop number unknown), chartered c.1923, was run initially by the Rev. Clarence Gifford. Mr. French joined the Troop as a Scout in 1927, eventually becoming Assistant Scoutmaster, then Scoutmaster. The Troop met in a house owned by Nathan Davis (of the Davis family that produced guns in Assonet), who every Christmas, would forgive the rent the Troop was supposed to have paid for use of the house as a meeting place. Around the beginning of World War II, Mr. Davis died and the Troop was evicted and began meeting in a building that was between the bridge on South Main Street and the building that is currently a gas station.

Mr. French told of long hikes to go camping (he said that a 14 mile hike was a rank requirement at the time) and being a time when most people had little money, many Scouts didn't get to go to summer camp as is common today. The boys would often camp under the stars (no tents) and each would carry with them; a hatchet, a knife, a clean tin can with some meal in it and an egg placed in the meal for protection, some meat and vegetables, and a frying pan. They would make "a sort of woodsman's stew, eating lunch and supper, but usually no breakfast". Some of the places the Troop would camp included the Milliken family farm in Dighton, some private land in Myricks, and on Red Gate farm off of Narrows Road. Girl Scouts had been using the property, but would not go there any more after an oil spill at an oil refinery that used to be in Fall River came upstream with the tide and fouled the area for a while.

During the 1930's, the Troop had a band and they played in front of a tavern on South Main Street (former Green Dragon?). The boys would take lessons from a music teacher from Fall River for $1.00 a week and get an instrument in the deal. After the tavern closed and torn down, the Troop raised money, purchased the land, filled in the cellar hole and got the town to accept it as a park. The WPA (Work Projects Administration) rebuilt the band stand. Some professional musicians would play with the band just for fun; nobody got paid except the band leader, Mr. Leo Vezina.

According to Mr. Art Blaise, long associated with East Freetown's Troop 64, Boy Scouts in Freetown and Assonet were pressed into service fighting a forest fire in 1943.

Current Boy Scout Troop 164 was chartered in 1997 by K.R.R. Inc. with five boys, Gary Vander Kaaden as Scoutmaster and Mark Logan as Assistant Scoutmaster.

Meeting initially at the United Church of Assonet, and building steadily, the Troop size reached 26 at one point. Other adults who are or have been involved, holding at various times position of Assistant Scoutmaster and/or Troop Committee member are; Jeanne Vander Kaaden, Jimmie Hunter and his late wife Carol, who was Committee Chair for many years, Eric Flanders, Barb Flanders, Steve Quinlan, Jeannie Quinlan, Tim Quinlan, Ray Mosher, Jackie Mosher, Mike McCue, Mike Logan, Charles Cavallaro, Donald Violette, Vince Kyne and Matthew Paquin. After Cub Scout Pack 164 rechartered at St. Bernard, Mr. Logan asked K.R.R. Inc. to release its' charter on the Troop so that it could charter through St. Bernard in order to align itself with the Pack. Troop 164 now meets at St. Bernard on Thursday nights from the beginning of September to the end of May.

The Troop has attended Summer Camp every year at Cachalot Scout Reservation in Carver, MA and won many awards at the annual "Klondike Derby" held there in winter (Scouts pull a sled full of gear around camp to compete against other troops in Scout skills). Many camping trips, including camporees (camping trips attended by multiple Troops, usually with a theme, and facilities set up for Scouts to earn several merit badges) and lots of hiking have been standard fare for the Troop from the start. The Troop attended the Jersey Shores Council's annual invitational camporee on the grounds of Six Flags New Jersey three times (2000, 2002 and 2004). Of course, a Boy Scout Troop wouldn't be complete without community service; Troop 164 has, among other things cleaned up trash at Porter Pasture, the town beach, and Hathaway Park.

The most involved community service projects are "Eagle Projects" a requirement of earning the rank of Eagle Scout, and six young men from Troop 164 have so far earned this highest honor in Scouting. Jono Vander Kaaden, Zack Flanders, and Mike McCue all earned theirs on July 20, 2004, facing an Eagle Board of Review while at Summer Camp. Their Eagle Projects were respectively; replacing (including painting) the fence on the side of the United Church of Assonet, a coat drive that included collecting, sorting and distribution of over 200 coats, and clearing of overgrowth of one of several long forgotten cemeteries discovered during the clearing of the land for the Stop & Shop distribution center. On July 21, 2005, Tim Quinlan earned the rank; his Eagle Project was organizing and orchestrating a blood drive held at the Berkley Community School. On April 11, 2007, Mike Logan attained the rank; his project was to clear another of the cemeteries at the Stop & Shop property. Lastly, but certainly not to be the last, on July 11, 2007, Alex Mosher became an Eagle Scout. His project was to clear overgrowth from the walking trail on conservation property known as Puddingstone Preserve (across from Friend Street on South Main), and erect a kiosk at the entrance with a locus map.

Eagle Scouts from Troop 164 Assonet

Zachary P. Flanders	07/27/04
Michael Sean Logan	04/11/07
Michael T. McCue	07/27/04
Alex Brendan Mosher	07/11/07
Timothy Steven Quinlan	07/21/05
Jonathan M. Vander Kaaden	07/27/04

CREW 82 WESTPORT

The first charter for Crew 82 Westport was issued on July 3, 2006. The unit is sponsored by a Group of Citizens. The crew was the brainchild of Eagle Scout Marc C. Gallant (Troop 6 Bristol) who had been a German WWII re-enactor from the age of 14 and is comprised of fellow re-enactors. The members of the unit live in various areas in Massachusetts, Connecticut and Vermont, so regular meeting are held in Yahoo groups via the internet. The Crew gets together regularly to camp at our Scout reservations and never fails to draw a crowd as they practice drilling and maneuvers with their authentic WWII gear and equipment.

A highlight of the Venturing Crew's short tenure was in October of 2007 when Crew President, Marc Gallant, organized and ran a duel district camporee at Fort Adams in Newport, RI. The Pokanoket/Massasoit camporee was titled "Remembering World War II" and featured themed station activities, a SPAM (the meat that won the war) cook-off and two battles to regain the Fort which was "occupied" by the Germans when the Scouts arrived. Of course, American forces were victorious in the end and historical news reels declaring victory were shown. The event was attended by more than 450 scouts and adults.

In March of 2008, a casting call was issued by Martin Scorsese for German WWII re-enactors for a new film called Shutter Island starring Leonardo DiCaprio. Two members of Crew 82, President Marc Gallant and Matthew Guertin were called to be "extras" in the movie. As filming progressed, both young men were asked to do additional screen work. Marc was even called to film a scene with Leonardo DiCaprio in which he is murdered by Leo. The film is due to be released in February 2010.

The Advisors of Crew 82 Westport: Diane J. Cloutier 2006-
The Presidents of Crew 82: Marc C. Gallant 2006-

TROOP 82 PROVIDENCE

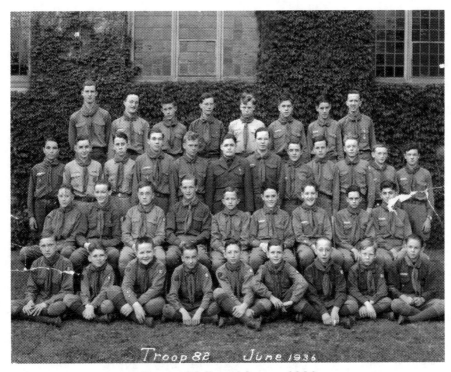

Troop 82 Providence 1936
Donald C. Dewing, Scoutmaster—(second row from the top in the middle)

Troop 82 Providence was founded in 1927 by Donald C. Dewing. Don served as Scoutmaster from the day he founded the unit until the day he passed away in December of 1988. Don was Troop 82's fabulous and only Scoutmaster for its first 61 years, though he always shared credit with a great succession of assistants . . . such great leaders as F. P. Drummond, Harvey Sanborn, Herb and Art Nelson, Grant Dulgarian, John Cashman, Bob Carlson and Dick Donnelly. While Donald himself had become only a Star Scout, he made Life and Eagle again and again through the 109 proud Scouts who reached the rank of Eagle while Don was their Scoutmaster. When Donald retired as an Assistant Secretary of Amica Insurance Company in 1972, he came to work full time at Scout Headquarters. He was Treasurer of the Narragansett Council from 1955 to 1985 and Treasurer of the Rhode Island Boy Scouts from 1950 until his death in 1988. A Regional Award he received describes Don accurately: *"His contribution to Scouting can never be measured. No man possesses the spirit of Scouting as does Donald Dewing. He lives and breathes the program 24 hours a day. His heart and soul have been to carry out the Scout Oath and Law to their fullest meaning"*. Truer words have never been spoken. Once Donald passed, Troop 82 under the able guidance of Bob Carlson and Ronalds Platt made it through another ten years but dropped in 1999.

Troop 82 Providence's 119 Eagle Scouts

Daniel Ackroyd	1990	Stephen Goldstein	1972
Fred W. Ackroyd	1944	Paul A. Good	1974
James Ackroyd	1960	Richard H. Gray	1948
Joseph Jacob Ackroyd	1993	Donald T. Hazard	1944
Luke Joshua Ackroyd	1989	William B. Hendee	1986
Peter I. Alberg	1986	Richard W. Horton	1934
Marc D. Aneyci	1984	Warren R. Howard	1942
Erving T. Arnold, Jr.	1941	John C. Hurd	1942
Robert M. Bannon	1950	Joseph A. Ilacqua, Jr.	1984
Harvey M. Bernstein	1932	Phillip R. Karlson	1988
Larry Bernstein	1976	David K. Kay	1982
Evan R. Berube	1980	Paul B. Kerr	1937
Mark A. Berube	1978	Charles W. Killam	1941
Robert A. Bishop	1934	Richard C. Knight	1937
George Turner Blome	1947	Jonathan A. Kosterlitz	1993
William Arnold Blome	1943	Bill Leonard	1965
Herbert H. Boden, Jr.	1938	Alan Jay Leven	1974
Michael N. Botvin	1957	Robert L. Linne	1948
William E. Boyle, Jr.	1954	Melvin A. Lipson	1950
E. Everett Brunnckow	1941	Stanley Livingston, III	1968
John M. Campbell	1943	Ronald T. Marshall	1980
Daniel C. Card	1985	Richard A. Matthews	1948
Donald R. Carlson	1977	Campbell McGreen	1937
Roger D. Carpenter	1947	Henry McGreen	1943
Samuel J. Cashman	1942	John McGreen	1940
Patrick F. Clarkin	1992	David McKendry	1957
John A. Comery	1971	Donald B. McKendry	1957
William J. Comery	1967	James R. McKendry, Jr.	1950
William E. Costello	1938	Paul R. McLaughlin	1976
Channing H. Cox	1936	Charles McTammany, Jr.	1932
Anthony Reis DeMoura	1988	William Millam	1941
John J. Dee	1936	Stephen Miller	1960
Sean F. Donnelly	1980	Richard F. Morgan	1933
William C. Dorgan	1942	Edwin F. Morgan, Jr.	1932
John J. Dorgan, Jr.	1938	Kenneth J. Morrill	1979
James C. Dorian	1962	Michael V. O'Connell	1990
James C. Dorian, Jr.	1985	Edward Alexander Orloff	1998
Ethan Dubois	1971	Thomas J. W. Parker	1996

Grant D. Dulgarian	1962	Wesley Perkins	1971
Stephen P. Ellis	1963	Rhodes Raymond	1928
Theodore I. Ellis, III	1957	Robert W. Raymond	1952
Calvin Fisher, Jr.	1935	Thomas F. Riley	1983
Andrew M. Frutchey	1995	Kenneth F. Sargent	1969
Robert F. Gammons	1935	Peter Scheidler, Jr.	1995
Steven Goldsmith	1962	Alan D. Schinazi	1984

Troop 82 Providence's 119 Eagle Scouts Continued

Robert G. Schinazi	1984	Norman C. Taylor	1941
Robert R. Scholdan	1983	Stanley M. Taylor	1937
David J. Scoliard	1985	Geb W. Thomas	1981
John A. Shannon	1965	John T. Toher	1936
Marc Alan Silverman	1972	Eugene F. Tortolani	1945
David Singbnad	1982	Edward Tower	1957
Richard Skelly	1947	Francis L. Warren	1942
Robert Speaker	1973	Robert Warren	1943
Philip A. Speare	1984	Christopher R. Watson	1984
Kevin S. Stevens	1985	Edward Whittingslow	1955
Doublas Stewart	1927	Thomas Whittingslow	1954
Benjamin R. Strauss	1988	Charles R. Williams	1935
Edward I. Swanson	1939	David C. Wooman, PhD	1959
Robert Swanson	1946	Matthew M. Zalk	1981
		Edward H. Ziegler, IV	1984

AN INTERESTING STORY ABOUT TWO RHODE ISLAND GOVERNORS

The Honorable John H. Chafee and the Honorable Bruce Sundlun were schoolboy pals on the East Side of Providence and both were members of Boy Scout Troop 38. During the winter of 1933, the troop went on a cold-weather campout in Rockville, Rhode Island, at Camp Yawgoog. The Scouts were playing a spirited game of ice hockey on Yawgoog Pond when they heard an ominous creaking sound. Suddenly, one of them fell through the ice. He struggled to keep from going under in the frigid water. While most of his companions raced off in search of help, his pal remained. Recalling the Scoutmaster's training, the 11-year old lay flat on the ice and edged slowly toward his friend, pushing his hockey stick out ahead. "Grab the stick!" he yelled. His friend got hold of the stick. The rescuer moved slowly back over the groaning ice until he had pulled his shivering friend onto the lakeshore. When the other Scouts returned with their leaders, they wrapped the wet Scout in blankets and rushed him to the hospital, where he was pronounced none the worse for his experience. The rescuer went on to graduate from Yale and Harvard Law School, fought with the Marines in World War II and Korea and came home to serve three terms as governor of Rhode Island (1963 to 1969). His name is John Chafee. The boy he rescued graduated from Williams College and also got his law degree from Harvard. He survived being shot down over France in World War II, made a successful career in business, and served two terms as governor of Rhode Island (1991 to 1995). His name is Bruce Sundlun. From opposing political parties, in a state where such things matter, the two have remained friends. Chafee, the rescuer, seldom mentions the incident and discourages discussion of it. Sundlun, the rescued, seizes the opportunity to discuss it. "While others panicked," he said, "John Chafee remained cool. If he had not, I would not be here to tell the tale".

INTERESTING FACTS ABOUT
The Rhode Island Boy Scouts and
Narragansett Council, Boy Scouts of America

From 1910 to 1921, the Rhode Island Boy Scouts used the terminology 'Office of the Chairman of the Board of Directors' rather than 'President'. That terminology was abolished by change of RIBS Bylaws in 1921. From 1910 thru 1915, the term 'Chief Scout' was used rather than 'Scout Executive'. The term 'Scout Executive' began in 1916 when Donald C. North became the first real paid executive of the organization.

The first Scout Headquarters was in Room 14 of the Journal Building in Providence. In the 1920's the Providence Journal needed more space so Scouting Headquarters moved to the Strand Building. In the early 30's Scouting Headquarters moved to 100 North Main Street, Providence, in a building strictly for social agencies. The growth of Scouting in the late 30's forced the move to 26 Custom House Street. In the 50's the building would be torn down and we moved to the Caesar Misch Building at 51 Empire Street and remained there until the new Council Service Center was completed in 1964. In 2004, the 175 Broad Street Headquarters was sold and Scout Headquarters moved to 10 Risho Avenue in East Providence, Rhode Island and is still leasing this space at the writing of this history.

Congress chartered the Boy Scouts of America on June 15th, 1916, and the Rhode Island Boy Scouts voted to merge with the Boy Scouts of America in May, 1917 but the Rhode Island Boy Scouts retained its corporate identity and the operating body became known as the Greater Providence Council, Boy Scouts of America.

First, It Was Called Rhode Island Boy Scouts

Rhode Island Boy Scouts was first organized as a voluntary association on September 6th, 1910. On April 13th, 1911, it was chartered under state laws for the purpose of giving boys of Rhode Island an organization in which they could be formed into groups that mirrored the newly formed National Boy Scout Program.

From 1910 to 1917, Rhode Island Boy Scouts established groups (Troops) throughout Rhode Island, except in Newport, Blackstone Valley and Woonsocket. In these locations, Troops were organized and affiliated with the National Council Boy Scouts of America.

Then Came Greater Providence Council

In 1917, Rhode Island Boy Scouts "merged" with the National movement. Under the terms of the agreement, the Greater Providence Council Boy Scouts of America was formed to take over the operation of the Scouting Program and supervision of Troops. The National Council Boy Scouts of America recognized the date of the Council's organization as September 6th, 1910, and granted all members back service to that date. The National Council Boy Scouts of America also agreed that the Rhode Island Boy Scouts could maintain its corporate identity so that it could continue to receive bequests, hold funds and properties and acquire other funds and properties in the future; thus, the formation of Rhode Island Boy Scouts as a Trustee organization.

Finally, the Merger of All Councils in Rhode Island

In 1929 and 1930, the Greater Providence Council Boy Scouts of America merged with the Newport County Council, the Pawtucket-Central Falls Council and the Woonsocket Council to form the Narragansett Council (#546) of the Boy Scouts of America.

2001—Another Merger

On July 1, 2001, the Moby Dick Council (#245) in New Bedford, Massachusetts, merged with the Narragansett Council adding 17 more cities and towns in Massachusetts to the 6 cities and towns the Narragansett Council was already serving. This merger also added the beautiful 900-acre Camp Cachalot in the Myles Standish State Forest to our current seven camping properties and five more employees to the Narragansett Council family.

Over 100 Years of Continuous Service
Although in 2012, Narragansett Council is only celebrating its 83rd year of chartered existence under this name, in reality, it has been providing over 100 continuous years of service to the youth of Rhode Island and parts of Massachusetts and Connecticut.

SCOUT EXECUTIVES AND THE YEARS THEY SERVED

1910-1911	Adj. Gen. Charles W. Abbot, Jr., Chief Scout
1912-1913	Col. Harry Cutler, Chief Scout
1914	Frank B. McSoley, Chief Scout & President
1915	Arthur L. Lake, Chief Scout & President
1916-1917	Donald C. North—first Paid Scout Executive
1918	Raymond W. Seamans (Only served for part of the year)
1918-1962	J. Harold Williams (Referred to as 'Chief')
1962-1972	Robert F. Parkinson
1973-1990	Vincent N. Borrelli
1990-1993	Roy L. Williams
1993-1999	Lyle K. Antonides
2000-2011	David S. Anderson
2012-	John H. Mosby

RHODE ISLAND BOY SCOUTS PRESIDENTS

1910-1913 & 1916-1917	Charles E. Mulhearn		
1918-1919	George L. Gross	1927-1969	T. Dawson Brown
1920-1921	N. Stuart Campbell	1969-1996	Paul C. Nicholson, Jr.
1922-1926	William B. MacColl	1996-	Jonathan K. Farnum

Scouting's Leadership from 1910 to Present

Year	President	Year	Commissioner
1910-1913	Charles E. Mulhearn	1910	G. Edward Buxton, Jr.
1914	Frank B. McSoley	1911-1917	John R. Rathom
1915	Arthur L. Lake	1918-1919	G. Edward Buxton
1916-1917	Charles E. Mulhearn	1920	H. Anthony Dyer
1918-1921	T. F. I. McDonnell	1921	E. S. Chaffee
1922	N. Stuart Campbell	1922-1924	Donald S. Babcock
1923-1926	William B. MacColl	1925	William G. Vinal
1927-1932	T. Dawson Brown	1926-1930	F.C. Pearce Drummond
1933-1937	F.C. Pearce Drummond	1931-1932	Albert E. Lownes
1938-1940	William B. Spencer	1933-1935	Donald North
1941-1943	Albert E. Lownes	1936-1938	Fred W. Marvel
1944-1946	Jeremiah E. O'Connell	1939-1947	Timothy E. O'Neil
1947-1948	Elmer S. Horton	1948-1957	Jeremiah E. O'Connell
1949-1950	David S. Seaman	1958-1961	Wilford S. Budlong
1951-1952	James L. Hanley	1962-1964	William J. Gilbane
1953-1954	Wilford S. Budlong	1975-1979	Michele DeCiantis
1955-1956	Roger T. Clapp	1980-1984	Jules A. Cohen
1957-1958	Paul C. Nicholson, Jr.	1985-1987	Arthur W. Keegan
1959-1960	William J. Gilbane	1988-1990	Robert Barnes
1961	W. Chesley Worthington	1991-1993	Charles A. Bennett
1962-1963	Aaron H. Roitman	1994-1996	Nikki M. Dziadosz
1964-1965	Phillips D. Booth	1997	Theodore F. Jakubowski
1966-1968	John A. Horton	1998-2000	Robert Barnes
1969-1970	Louis R. Hampton	2001-2004	Roger G. Cardin
1971-1972	Charles E. Clapp II	2005-2008	Frank Ferraro
1973-1975	Jacques E. Dubois	2009-2010	William A. Taylor
1976-1978	George B. Roorbach	2011-	John A. Gilmore, Jr.

1979-1982	Stanley F. Turco
1983-1984	Herbert W. Cummings
1985-1988	Jules A. Cohen
1989-1991	Jonathan K. Farnum
1992-1994	Paul J. Choquette, Jr.
1995-1997	Robert J. Sirhal
1998-1999	Andrew M. Erickson
2000-2002	Robert H. Pease, Jr.
2003-2005	Joseph P. Gencarella
2006-2007	Michael A. Lee
2008-2009	Robert A. DiMuccio
2010-2012	Andrew C. Hewitt
2013-	George W. Shuster

BSA MISSION

The mission of the Boy Scouts of America is to prepare young people to make ethical and moral choices over their lifetimes by instilling in them the values of the Scout Oath and Law.

BSA VISION

The Boy Scouts of America will prepare every eligible youth in America to become a responsible, participating citizen and leader who is guided by the Scout Oath and Law.

SCOUT OATH

On my honor I will do my best
To do my duty to God and my country
and to obey the Scout Law;
To help other people at all times;
To keep myself physically strong,
Mentally awake and morally straight.

SCOUT LAW

Trustworthy	Obedient
Loyal	Cheerful
Helpful	Thrifty
Friendly	Brave
Courteous	Clean
Kind	Reverent

DESCRIPTION & TRANSLATION OF
NARRAGANSETT COUNCIL'S SHOULDER PATCH
DESIGNED IN 2002 BY FRED EDDINS

THE SUNRISE—Represents the future of Scouting.

THE BRIDGE—The bridge to the future of Narragansett Council Scouting (Drawing based on the Newport Bridge, center of Narragansett Council area.)

THE SAILBOAT—Representing our trip through Scouting from the past and sailing into the future. The sailboat is based on the great sailboat *Reliance* of the America's Cup fame. The *Reliance* was built and raced in 1903 the same year that Baden Powell, after reviewing the Boys Brigade, was inspired to start the Boy Scouts. (The name '*Reliance*' represents the Scouts 'reliance' to uphold the law and oath.)

THE WHITE WHALE'S TAIL—A symbol of the merger of the Moby Dick Council and the Narragansett Council.

THE TWO STARS—Truth and knowledge.